Crossway Bible Guide

Series Editors: Ian Coffey (NT), Stephen Gaukroger (OT)
New Testament Editor: Steve Motyer

Titles in this series

Genesis, Richard and Tricia Johnson
Exodus, Stephen Dray
Leviticus, Derek Tidball
Joshua, Charles Price
Ruth and Esther, Debra Reid
Ezra and Nehemiah, Dave Cave
Psalms 1 – 72, Alan Palmer
Psalms 73 – 150, Alan Palmer and Debra Reid
Isaiah, Philip Hacking
Six Minor Prophets, Michael Wilcock
Haggai, Zechariah and Malachi, John James
Matthew's Gospel, Stephen Dray
Mark's Gospel, David Hewitt
Luke's Gospel, Simon Jones
John's Gospel, Ian Barclay
Acts, Stephen Gaukroger
Romans, David Coffey
1 Corinthians, Robin Dowling and Stephen Dray
2 Corinthians, Jonathan Lamb
Ephesians, Steve Motyer
Philippians, Ian Coffey
Colossians and Philemon, Stephen Gaukroger and
Derek Wood
1 & 2 Thessalonians, Alec Motyer and Steve Motyer
Timothy and Titus, Michael Griffiths
James, David Field
1 Peter, Andrew Whitman

The Bible with Pleasure, Steve Motyer
Discovering the New Testament, Simon Jones
Housegroups: The Leaders' Survival Guide, Ian Coffey and
Stephen Gaukroger (eds.)
Rebuild, Fran Beckett (ed.)

Colossians and Philemon:
Crossway Bible Guide

Stephen Gaukroger
Derek Wood

Crossway Books Leicester

CROSSWAY BOOKS
38 De Montfort Street, Leicester LE1 7GP, England

First published 2002

British Library Cataloguing in Publication Data
A catalogue record for this book is available from the British Library.

ISBN 1–85684–208–8

Set in Palatino

Typeset in Great Britain by Avocet Typeset, Brill, Aylesbury, Bucks
Printed in Great Britain by Omnia Books Ltd, Glasgow

With love to our friends at
Gold Hill Baptist Church
and St Michael's, Waddington

CONTENTS

Three routes through Colossians and Philemon   9
Welcome!   11
How to use this Bible Guide   12
    How to tackle personal Bible study   12
    How to tackle your group Bible study   13
    What can we expect to learn from Colossians?   16
    What can we expect to learn from Philemon?   16
Finding your way around this book   17
Map   19

Colossians in a nutshell   20

1 Christ in you, the hope of glory
  Meet the key players 1:1–2   22
    Where was Colosse?   24
  Encouragement for the church 1:3–8   25
    Hope, our heavenly anchor   28
  Prayer requests 1:9–14   29
  The uniqueness of Christ 1:15–20   33
    Fullness   36
  The wonder of salvation 1:21–23   37
  The task of ministry 1:24–29   39
    The mystery of the gospel   42

2 Do not be led astray from Christ
  The purpose of Paul's ministry:
  a strong church 2:1–5   44
    The heart   46
    'Present with you in spirit'   47

The battle between empty false teaching
and fullness in Christ 2:6–12   48
   Subtle deceptions   51
Three enemies defeated 2:13–15   52
   Confronting error   55
Three imposters exposed 2:16–23   56
   Fasting   59

3 Live holy lives in Christ
The battle for the mind 3:1–4   62
   Manipulating your beliefs   64
Killing off the old life 3:5–7   65
   The wrath of God   69
The true equality 3:8–11   71
New clothes for a new lifestyle 3:12–14   74
Live thankfully as the people of God 3:15–17   78
Personal relationships 3:18 – 4:1   82
   Paul and women   85
   Christian households   87

4 Make Christ widely known
The priority of prayer 4:2–4   90
   Prayer: a combined operation   93
Living the good news 4:5–6   95
Partners in the gospel 4:7–15   98
Final instructions and greeting 4:16–18   102

Philemon
Who was Philemon?   106
Greetings and thanksgiving 1–7   107
   'The church that meets in your home' 110
Paul's urgent plea for Onesimus 8–21   111
   Paul and slavery   114
Farewell 22–25   115
   From useless slave to bishop?   118

For further reading   119

Three routes through Colossians and Philemon

If you are planning a series of Bible studies, here are three examples of selections, each involving eight studies.

1. **A bird's-eye look at Colossians**

   1:15–20   The uniqueness of Christ, p. 33
   1:24–29   The task of ministry, p. 39
   2:6–12   The battle between empty false teaching and fullness in Christ, p. 48
   2:13–15   Three enemies defeated, p. 52
   3:8–11   The true equality, p. 71
   3:18 – 4:1   Personal relationships, p. 82
   4:2–4   The priority of prayer, p. 90
   4:5–6   Living the good news, p. 95

2. **Pastoral care**
   Colossians

   1:3–8   Encouragement for the church, p. 25
   1:9–14   Prayer requests, p. 29
   1:24–29 The task of ministry, p. 39
   2:1–5   The purpose of Paul's ministry: a strong church, p. 44
   3:1–4   The battle for the mind, p. 62

   Philemon

   1–7   Greetings and thankgiving, p. 107
   8–21   Paul's urgent plea for Onesimus, p. 111
   22–25   Farewell, p. 115

3. Living out your faith

Colossians

3:1–4   The battle for the mind, p. 62
3:5–7   Killing off the old life, p. 65
3:8–11   The true equality, p. 71
3:12–14   New clothes for a new lifestyle, p. 74
3:15–17   Live thankfully as the people of God, p. 78
3:18 – 4:1 Personal relationships, p. 82
4:2–4   The priority of prayer, p. 90
4:5–6   Living the good news, p. 95

Welcome!

These days, meeting together to study the Bible in groups appears to be a booming leisure-time activity in many parts of the world. In the United Kingdom alone, it is estimated that over one million people each week meet in home Bible-study groups.

This series has been designed to help such groups and, in particular, those who lead them. These Bible Guides are also very suitable for individual study, and may help hard-pressed preachers, teachers and students too (see 'How to use this Bible Guide', opposite).

We have therefore enlisted authors who are in the business of teaching the Bible to others and are doing it well. They have kept in their sights two clear aims:

1. To explain and apply the message of the Bible in non-technical language.
2. To encourage discussion, prayer and action on what the Bible teaches.

All of us engaged in the project believe that the Bible is the Word of God – given to us in order that people might discover him and his purposes for our lives. We believe that the sixty-six books which go to make up the Bible, although written by different people, in different places, at different times, through different circumstances, have a single unifying theme: that theme is Salvation. This means free forgiveness and the removal of all our guilt, it means the gift of eternal life, and it means the wholeness of purpose and joy which God has designed us to experience here and now, all of this being made possible through the Lord Jesus Christ.

How to use this Bible Guide

These guides have been prepared both for personal study and for the leaders and members of small groups. More information about group study follows on the next few pages.

You can use this book very profitably as a personal study guide. The short studies are ideal for daily reading: the first of the questions provided is usually aimed to help you with personal reflection (see 'How to tackle personal Bible study', below). If you prefer to settle down to a longer period of study, you can use groups of three to five studies, and thus get a better overview of a longer Bible passage. In either case, using the Bible Guide will help you to be disciplined about regular study, a habit that countless Christians have found greatly beneficial. (See also 'Three routes through Colossians and Philemon' on pages 9–10 for methods of selecting studies if you do not intend to use them all.)

Yet a third use for these Bible Guides is as a quarry for ideas for the busy Bible teacher, providing outlines and application for those giving talks or sermons or teaching children. You will need more than this book can offer, of course, but the way the Bible text is broken down, comments are offered and questions are raised may well suggest directions to follow.

How to tackle personal Bible study

We have already suggested that you might use this book as a personal study guide. Now for some more detail.

One of the best methods of Bible study is to read the text through carefully several times, if possible using different versions or translations. Having reflected on the material, it is a good discipline to write down your own thoughts before doing anything else. At this stage it can be useful to consult another background book. See 'Resources' on page 14 and 'For further reading' on page 119. If you are using this book as your main study resource, then read through the relevant sections carefully, turning up the Bible references that are mentioned. The questions at the end of each chapter are specifically designed to help you to apply the passage to your own situation. You may find it helpful to write your answers to the questions in your notes.

It is a good habit to conclude with prayer, bringing before God the things you have learned.

If this kind of in-depth study is too demanding for you and you have only a short time at your disposal, read the Bible passage, read the comments in the Bible Guide, think round one of the questions and commit what you have learned to God in a brief prayer. This would take about fifteen minutes without rushing it.

How to tackle your group Bible study

1. Getting help

If you are new to leading groups, you will obviously want to get all the help you can from ministers and experienced friends. Books are also extremely helpful and we strongly recommend a book prepared by the editors of this series of Bible Guides: *Housegroups: The Leaders' Survival Guide*, edited by Ian Coffey and Stephen Gaukroger (Crossway Books, 1996). This book looks at the whole range of different types of group, asking what is the point of it all, what makes a good leader, how to tackle your meeting, how to help the members, how to study, pray, share and worship, and plenty of other pointers, tips and guidelines.

This book is a 'must' for all leaders of small groups. It is written by a team of people widely experienced in this area. It is available at your local Christian bookshop. If you have difficulty in obtaining a copy, write to Crossway Books, Norton Street, Nottingham NG7 3HR, UK.

2. Planning a programme with your Bible Guide

This guide is a commentary on God's Word, written to help group members to get the most out of their studies. Although it is never ideal to chop up Scripture into small pieces, which its authors never intended, huge chunks are indigestible and we have tried to provide a diet of bite-sized mouthfuls.

The book is divided into major parts, each with a title indicated by a part-title page with a large number. If you want to get an overview of Colossians in a series of meetings you will need to select appropriate studies for each meeting. Read them yourself first and prepare a short summary of the studies you are tackling for your group. Ideally you could write it on a sheet of A5 paper and hand a copy to each member. Then choose one study from the part you are dealing with as a basis for your meeting. Do not attempt to pack more than one study into one meeting but choose the crucial one, the study which best crystallizes the message.

If you do not intend to cover the whole of Colossians, choose a series of studies to suit the number of meetings you have available. Each part of the commentary is divided into a few (usually 3–6) studies. It is a good idea to use consecutive studies, not to dodge about. You will then build up a detailed picture of one section of Scripture. Alternative examples of programmes of study for these two letters are given in 'Three routes through Colossians and Philemon' on pages 9–10.

3. Resources

You will find any or all of these books of great value in providing background to your Bible knowledge. Put some of them on your Christmas list and build up your library.

New Bible Dictionary or *New Concise Bible Dictionary* (IVP)
New Bible Atlas (IVP)

New Bible Commentary (21st Century edition) (IVP)
Handbook of Life in Bible Times, John Thompson (IVP)
The Bible User's Manual (IVP)
The Lion Handbook to the Bible (Lion Publishing)
The Message of the Bible (Lion Publishing)
NIV *Study Bible* (Hodder & Stoughton)
The Bible with Pleasure, Steve Motyer (Crossway Books)
Discovering the New Testament, Simon Jones (Crossway
  Books)

The relevant volume in the IVP Tyndale Commentary
series will give you reliable and detailed help with any
knotty points you may encounter.

4. Preparing to lead

Reading, discussing with friends, studying, praying,
reflecting on life ... preparation can be endless. But do not
be daunted by that. If you wait to become the perfect
leader you will never start at all. The really vital elements
in preparation are:

▶ prayer (not only in words but an attitude of dependence on God: 'Lord, I can't manage this on my own')

▶ familiarity with the study passage (careful reading of
  the text, the Bible Guide study and any other resource
  books that throw light on it) and

▶ a clear idea of where you hope to get in the meeting
  (notes on your introduction, perhaps, recap what was
  covered at the last meeting, and what direction you
  hope the questions will take you in – don't force the
  group to give your answers).

Here is a short checklist for the busy group leader:

Have I prayed about the meeting?
Have I decided exactly what I want to achieve
  through the meeting?
Have I prepared the material?

Am I clear about the questions that will encourage positive group discussion?

Am I gently encouraging silent members?

Am I, again gently, quietening the chatterers?

Am I willing to admit ignorance?

Am I willing to listen to what the group members say and to value their contributions?

Am I ready not to be dogmatic, not imposing my ideas on the group?

Have I planned how to involve the members in discovering for themselves?

Have I developed several 'prayer points' that will help focus the group?

Are we applying Scripture to our experience of real life or only using it as a peg to hang our opinions on?

Are we finding resources for action and change or just having a nice talk?

Are we all enjoying the experience together?

What can we expect to learn from Colossians?

▶ How to put Christ first in our lives

▶ How to resist the temptation to be swept away by exciting new teaching

▶ How to avoid superstition in all its forms

▶ How to let our lifestyle live up to our faith-profession

▶ How to value our friends and work with them

What can we expect to learn from Philemon?

▶ How to be wise and tactful

▶ How to avoid confrontation and pursue reconciliation

▶ How to recognize and oppose slavery in all its modern forms

Finding your way around this book

In our Bible Guides we have developed special symbols to make things easier to follow. Every study therefore has an opening section which is the passage in a nutshell.

The main section is the one that *makes sense of the passage.*

Questions

Every passage also has special questions for personal and group study after the main section. Some questions are addressed to us as individuals, some speak to us as members of our church or home group, while others concern us as members of God's people worldwide. The questions are deliberately designed

▶ to get people thinking about the passage

▶ to apply the text to 'real-life' situations

▶ to encourage reflection, discussion and action!

As a group leader you may well discover additional questions that will have special relevance to your group, so look out for these and note them in your preparation time.

Digging deeper

Some passages require an extra amount of explanation, and we have put these sections into two categories. The first kind gives additional background material that helps us to understand something factual. For example, if we dig deeper into the Gospels, it helps us to know who the Pharisees were, so that we can see more easily why they related to Jesus in the way they did. These technical sections are marked with a spade.

Important doctrines

The second kind of background section appears with passages which have important doctrines contained in them and which we need to study in more depth if we are to grow as Christians. Special sections that explain them to us are marked with a face as above.

Asia Minor in the time of Paul

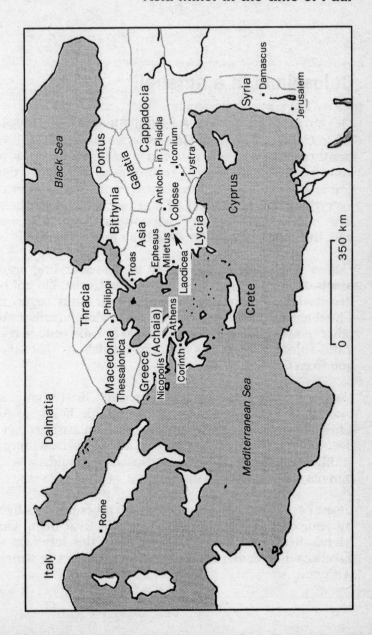

Colossians in a nutshell

Chapter 1. Greetings from Paul and Timothy to the believers in Colosse. We thank God for your faith and we constantly pray that he will give you wisdom, as you grow in knowledge of him and in fruitfulness. Remember that Christ is supreme. He was involved in the creation of everything and he holds it all together. All God's fullness lives in him. This 'mystery' we now proclaim. 'Christ in you, the hope of glory.' So we all aim for perfection.

Chapter 2. Do not be led astray by fine-sounding arguments. Continue to be rooted firmly in Christ. Do not be deceived by hollow philosophies. Your faith began in Christ and you need only Christ to develop it further. All other 'powers' are subject to him. Do not succumb to religious rules, superstitions or ritual regulations that sever you from Christ himself.

Chapter 3. Since you have been raised in Christ from your old life, let your new lifestyle reflect his holiness. All Christian believers are united because all barriers have been broken down at the cross. So live in peace with one another, especially wives with husbands, children with parents and slaves with masters.

Chapter 4. Keep on praying and enrich other people's lives by your conversation and the way you treat them. Our friends here send their greetings. Send this letter on to Laodicea. Remember my chains. May God's smile remain with you.

CHRIST IN YOU, THE HOPE OF GLORY

Colossians 1

Colossians 1:1–2

Meet the key players

Paul introduces himself in a tone of both authority and brotherly love.

Reading other people's letters from years ago is often fascinating, but it can also be frustrating because they are hard to understand. One of the reasons for this is that the writer leaves out a lot of what we want to know. His readers would know it already, so there was no need to say it. So some of our understanding of this letter to the church in Colosse will be the result of detective work, reconstructing the problems that Paul was addressing. We begin with the basics: who wrote to whom, where and where from?

From Paul the apostle and Timothy (verse 1)

Paul's name means 'little'. If this is significant it must refer to his height and not to his character. People of small stature are often more dynamic and determined than the gentler giants. He had been named Saul, but Acts 13:9 tells us that he was also called Paul, and that is the name he was to be known by.

He describes himself as 'an apostle of Christ Jesus'. The word 'apostle' was first used of a fleet of ships sent on a mission. It came to describe the commander of the fleet and eventually any messenger who had the authority of the one who sent him. The word 'apostle' appears about eighty times in the New Testament: a person sent with the authority of the one behind him, that is Christ Jesus. 'Christ' is the New Testament Greek equivalent of

'Messiah' or 'anointed one'. The name 'Jesus' means 'saviour'. 'You are to give him the name Jesus, because he will save his people from their sins,' said the angel to Joseph when he announced the Saviour's birth (Matthew 1:21). Thus Paul claims that he has been sent 'by the will of God', with the authority of no less than the Anointed One, the saviour of the world. This letter should be worth reading!

It comes jointly from Paul and Timothy. Timothy was one of Paul's leadership team, his young lieutenant. Paul was acting as his 'father in the faith' (look at 1 Timothy 1:2), his mentor or discipler, so he includes him in the greeting.

To the faithful in Christ (verse 2)

Of course, when Paul wrote 'brothers', he included brothers and sisters. The letter is addressed to the leaders of the church in the little market town of Colosse, but it is clear that Paul expected the whole church to read it or to hear it read.

Notice how they are described: 'holy and faithful'. Could we describe every member of our local church as 'holy and faithful'? In general, probably not. So was Paul engaging in a bit of apostolic flattery? No. He is not describing the spiritual tone of the church but stating a theological truth. These people are 'in Christ' and therefore they are holy. They are not perfect, sitting in neat rows and smiling toothpaste-ad smiles, without a problem in the world. No, they are holy as we are holy, in Christ, because his holiness brims over to include us. They are also 'faithful', faithful to the teachings of the apostles, following the sound tradition handed down to them from the teaching of Jesus himself, one generation on.

Grace and peace (verse 2)

The actual greeting comes now at the end of verse 2. 'Grace' is the undeserved love that God longs for us to accept. 'Peace' is that state of fellowship with him that Christ gives us by his Spirit. Paul is reminding his readers that because they are in the Son (Jesus) they share the same Father, God himself. So there's a kind of fraternal warmth between Paul and these people whom he's never even met. He has established his apostolic credentials, but he also affirms his love for them. So along with the pastoral warmth of this first section comes an unmistakable note of authority: 'I Paul, the apostle.' He is not boastful or arrogant, but is clearly stating that what is to follow will be God's message to the church in Colosse.

Questions

1. Where does authority come from? Make a list of possible answers, such as: the minister, because he/she is holy or because he/she is ordained; the membership body of the church; your denominational organization, the apostolic teaching in the Bible ... Which is basic to your church or fellowship? How does it work out in practice?
2. Can you claim to be 'holy and faithful'? In what sense? How can you become holier without being 'holier than thou'?
3. Think of examples of brotherly/sisterly love which exist between people who have never met one another. Share your experiences in the group. How can we deepen this love across cultures and geographical distances?

Where was Colosse?

Colosse was probably the least significant town that Paul ever wrote to. It was about a hundred miles inland from Ephesus in what is now Turkey (see map on page 19).

Colosse lay on a major commercial route that ran up the valley of the Lycus river. The soil was poor, so crops were difficult to grow, but sheep thrived and Colosse was known for the dye with which they processed the wool and marketed it all over the ancient world. In fact the colour 'Colosse', a deep blue, was a household word in the Roman Empire of the time. By the time of Paul's letter, however, the trade had diminished. Laodicea down the road had grown in importance and Colosse had become a small market town. Even the church there may not have seemed very significant, for when John wrote to the seven churches in that part of the world (Revelation 1 – 3) Colosse is not even mentioned. Yet this letter from Paul and his appeal to Philemon, who lived in Colosse, have put this little town on the map for all time.

Where was Paul when he wrote? He was clearly in prison (see 4:18). Some have claimed that he was in Caesarea in Palestine, some in Ephesus and others in Rome: quite a wide choice! Our understanding of the letter is not really influenced by where it came from, so we shall assume that Paul wrote from Rome at some date in the mid-50s AD.

Colossians 1:3–8

Encouragement for the church

The good news of the faith is the source of hope and encouragement.

Here is an ordinary cross-section of townsfolk who have turned to the faith of Christ, presented to them by one of their number, Epaphras (verses 7–8;

4:12). He, in his turn, had probably been led to the faith by Paul himself at Ephesus. But already false teaching was threatening to undermine their new-found faith, and Paul was bothered about them. He was no ivory-tower theologian, but a fellow-believer with a pastoral, caring heart. He could not leave his cell to come to them, but he could write.

'God' defined (verse 3)

Paul begins by thanking God for these believers; but which God? 'God' was a word used loosely in the ancient world, as it is today, with a small 'g' or a large 'G' or any size 'g' you wanted. Paul puts his credentials firmly on the table by stating that the God we love and worship is 'the Father of our Lord Jesus Christ'. In the pluralistic world of the twenty-first century, this is a timely reminder. Christians should not be slow to make clear that the only God worthy of that name is the Father of Jesus Christ.

Well done the Colossians! (verses 4–5)

So Paul thanks this God, the only God there is, for the Colossians' faith and their love for all believers. Here they were, miles from anywhere, yet he had heard about their faith and transformed lives. Perhaps they were particularly good at the ministry of hospitality. They had heard Epaphras preach, and didn't simply say, 'Yes, that's a doctrine we could believe'; they also said, 'Yes, that's a life we could live.'

What was it that moved these people so much that their beliefs spilled over into everyday loving and caring? In a word, it was the experience of 'hope'. The experience of hope powerfully lifted their spirits, energizing their very lives (see below). And this hope was not a vague wish, but was based on 'the word of truth, the gospel'. So our actions are inspired by what we believe, and our beliefs are confirmed by the hope that accompanies our actions in an endless cycle of fruitfulness and growth.

The gospel worldwide (verse 6)

This growth was happening all over the world, not just in Colosse. They were not alone. There was a little group of believers down the road in Laodicea; another at Lystra; another at Derbe; another in Antioch. All over the known world the gospel was bearing fruit. It may be annoying some people. People were being imprisoned for it, and even martyred for it, but the gospel was growing from small Galilean roots in a little Mediterranean land to a worldwide power. Wherever we are today, the roots of our faith can be traced back to the Holy Land in the Middle East. Tens of thousands of people are coming to Christ all over the world in nation after nation. In fact, Europe is a depressed backwater, almost a forgotten continent as far as church growth is concerned. In many countries the gospel is biting into cultures and societies and growing in spectacular fashion.

Epaphras the missionary (verses 7–8)

Church growth happens when people come to faith and understand that they cannot justify themselves or achieve merit that will qualify them for God's approval. It follows that real growth depends not on their powers of organization or even on their zeal, but on the initiative and power of God's Spirit. The key to this is to understand 'God's grace in all its truth' (verse 6), to learn to accept from God the gift that we cannot buy for ourselves: forgiveness and a wiping away of past wrongs. This is the gospel that the Colossians had heard from Epaphras and had gladly accepted.

Epaphras, as we have already mentioned, seems to have been a native of Colosse. He is one of the earliest examples of a national being trained to carry the gospel to his own people. He would have been at home with the customs and the dialects and tones of the language. He would have had inside information which would make him the ideal minister of Christ on Paul's behalf. His own people would have recognized him as someone they could trust. It is clear that Epaphras had kept Paul up to date with all the news from their church, and it was good news; their 'love in the Spirit'.

Questions

1. How can we make clear the meaning of the word 'God' to people who use it only as an oath and have no concept of God as we know him?
2. Is your church growing? In what ways? Why or why not?
3. Is the locally born missionary in the best position to carry the good news to the people he/she knows? Share your experiences, especially how you have managed when telling your own family what you believe.

Hope, our heavenly anchor

'Hope' is a very significant New Testament word. In verse 5 Paul reminds his readers that their faith and love for the saints (their fellow-believers) flow from their hope, just as a spring is the source of a river. Everything that Christians hold dear flows from this sense of hope. We hope in the truth, despite much evidence to the contrary. Wrong abounds on every side, the church is beleaguered and small, yet our hope is that God is in charge of his world. This is not mere wishful thinking: exclaiming, 'Oh goodness, I hope he is!' when the world seems out of control. It's a secure conviction that the destiny of this planet Earth is in God's hands, and that our future in heaven is guaranteed by the historical facts of the cross and resurrection and the 'seal' of the Holy Spirit that we have received.

The contrast between the world's hopes and the true Christian understanding of the word is nowhere clearer than in Ephesians 2:12: 'Remember that ... you were ...

without hope and without God in the world.' Whoever is without God is without hope. Only faith in God can give us a ground for hope, and that hope is secure and certain. The writer to the Hebrews describes it as an anchor for our souls (Hebrews 6:19), the source of our security, much more than a mere feeling of optimism.

In verse 27 Paul spotlights this hope – 'Christ in you, the hope of glory.' Glory? God's presence now, but also for the future, beyond death. 'If only for this life we have hope in Christ, we are to be pitied more than all men. But Christ has indeed been raised from the dead …' (1 Corinthians 15:19–20). Our hope is for now and eternity.

So the apostle calls this fledgling group of believers into a recognition of the hope that binds them together and gears them up for the future. It is secure in heaven. It's all there for you – provision for the future. 'Don't worry, little Colosse! Things might seem like hell now, and you may be incredibly pressured, but remember that heavenly anchor and live now in the knowledge of that certain future hope.'

Colossians 1:9–14

Prayer requests

When we pray we need to broaden our horizons. Prayer for specific and sometimes selfish matters needs to expand to daring to ask for greater wisdom and maturity for ourselves and others.

'For this reason' (verse 9), that is (Paul implies) 'because you have made such a good start on your life together as a Christian community, I pray earnestly that you will go on to greater maturity.' Paul knows that these people stand in need of strength and wisdom beyond their ordinary resources, so he makes this series of powerful prayer requests.

Pray the big prayers (verse 9)

Paul continually asks God to fill them 'with the knowledge of his will through all spiritual wisdom and understanding'. What a fantastic request! Sometimes in our prayers we get too shortsighted, focused only on Mrs Jones's bunion, the weather for the church picnic or some aspect of the church building. Yes, God wants us to pray about everything, however detailed, but we should remember the big prayers too for ourselves and our churches. Today we are desperately in need of people who are filled with knowledge and spiritual wisdom and insight. There's a delightful little phrase in the Old Testament about the tribe of Issachar, 'who understood the times and knew what Israel should do' (1 Chronicles 12:32). May we also be men and women of deep spiritual insight who understand our times and know what we should do.

Pleasing the Master (verse 10)

Paul's prayer continues, asking that the Colossians 'may live a life worthy of the Lord and may please him in every way'. It is not enough to be filled to the brim with wisdom and understanding if we do not put it into practice. Paul's idea of service is modelled on the ancient household, where, like a butler, one servant was in charge of the others. His job was to see that the master was well served, and he would be looking ahead all the time to see how he could please him, anticipating his master's needs. Paul asks God to help his people to anticipate their Master's needs almost before he asks.

Some of us are rather dense spiritually. We need God to hit us with a hammer to get our attention. Some kind of crisis may come to shake us up, to alert us to God's call. C. S. Lewis said that pain was God's megaphone. But it need not be pain – it could be intense pleasure. Think of being in love. When we are in love we try to please the beloved; nothing is too much trouble. Paul is saying in effect, 'You are in love with God in Christ. So go out of your way to please him. Then God will smile on everything you do as you bear fruit and grow in your knowledge of what he wants you to do.'

An ongoing momentum of glory (verses 11–12)

Paul's long and breathless sentence (seventy-eight words in the New International Version) carries us along with such excitement that it's difficult to grasp the full meaning of his prayer. Verses 11–12 go something like this: 'May you experience this glorious power because you need endurance to keep you going. You need to be patient because it's a long haul. But you need to be joyful too.' (There's nothing more depressing than someone who is miserably patient!) 'May you know joy and may you give thanks to the Father. Why? Because he has chosen you to share in his inheritance.' (So there's a will involved here. How do you receive the inheritance from a will? Someone has to die first. Jesus had died and released the benefits of his death to all humankind – the salvation of the world and our hope for the future.) No wonder Paul gets excited and waxes lyrical. Some of us are afraid of showing emotion, but then who said you had to be an iceberg to inherit the kingdom of God?

The kingdom of light (verses 13–14)

God's kingdom is the kingdom of light. Jesus told his disciples that he was the light of the world (John 9:5). What is so important about light? One of the great polar explorers, speaking about his travels, asked his audience, 'What does the word "polar" mean to you?' They suggested words such as 'cold', 'frozen', 'icy'. 'That's interesting,' he said. 'It shows that you have never been to a polar region. The thing that strikes you most forcibly when you've been there for six months is not the cold but the darkness. For half the year there is perpetual darkness, an unremitting darkness that can drive explorers almost mad.'

Paul is implying, 'You have emerged from the corporate madness of a darkened world through the death of Jesus. You have inherited his kingdom of light and are being set free; glory in all that you have.' Many of us are not thrilled about our salvation because we have not understood how deep was the darkness from which we were delivered. But what a glory that salvation is! We have been rescued from sin ('we have redemption') and we've had the slate wiped clean. All the dirt has gone and we can see by his glorious light.

Questions

1. How do you distinguish between anticipating God's will before he calls us, and doing our own thing first and asking God to bless us when we've done it?
2. Draw up an agenda for an ideal prayer meeting. Decide on a balance between praise, intercession and confession, and between the 'big' prayers (for wisdom and knowledge and strength) and the detailed ones (Mrs Jones's bunion). Would an agenda of this kind ensure a proper balance in our prayer, or would it stifle spontaneity? Which is more important? Why?
3. Make a list of the different uses and benefits of light (e.g. torches, floodlights, searchlights, streetlamps, bedside lights ...) How does each of these illuminate our understanding of God's kingdom of light?

Colossians 1:15–20

The uniqueness of Christ

Jesus Christ has always existed with and in the Father. It is this Jesus who has established unity between us and God.

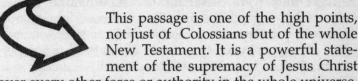 This passage is one of the high points, not just of Colossians but of the whole New Testament. It is a powerful statement of the supremacy of Jesus Christ over every other force or authority in the whole universe. Paul shows us Jesus as God's image, both the author and the purpose of creation. He has always existed, and is the one who reconciles his creation to God. These are mind-blowing ideas that need to be unpacked.

Jesus Christ is the image of God (verse 15)

There is no philosophical view, no force, no god even, nothing in the universe like Jesus. He is unique. Paul describes him as the image of the invisible God. Image can mean 'representation', like a monarch's or president's head on a coin. It can also mean 'manifestation': when you look at Jesus you see God. If you want to know what God is like, look at Jesus. He is the reflection of God, the mirror image. There are many words or illustrations we could use, but none of them gives us a complete picture. Basically, Jesus shows us God.

Jesus Christ is the author and purpose of creation (verses 16–17)

John's Gospel tells us that 'through him [the Word of God; that is, Jesus Christ] all things were made' (John 1:3). This does not mean that Jesus on his own created the universe, but that he was, as it were, God's agent. 'All things', says Paul here, 'were created by [means of] him and for him' (verse 16). He is, astonishingly, not just the originator but also the goal of all there is.

Now what are these thrones, powers, rulers and authorities that Paul speaks of? His readers probably knew exactly what he was getting at, but the ideas are unfamiliar to us. Perhaps some of these powers were positions adopted by earthly rulers and governments. Perhaps they were hierarchies of supernatural bodies, beloved by pagan religions. But we need not trouble ourselves with the details. Paul's point is that whatever kind of power you can think of, natural or supernatural, Jesus Christ existed before it and is superior to it. It is all included in the universe he was instrumental in creating.

Paul even goes one step further. Not only was Jesus the beginning and will be the end, but everything depends on him for its continuing existence now. 'In him all things hold together' (verse 17). If it were not for him, everything would fly apart and disintegrate. Physicists are searching for the ultimate principle at the root of everything. Need we look further?

Jesus Christ has always existed (verse 18)

Jesus is twice described as 'the firstborn' (verses 15, 18). Some of the cults, perhaps in the first century, and certainly in the twenty-first, have assumed that Jesus was a created being, inferior to God because the Father was there first and, as it were, 'produced' him. 'Firstborn' can mean 'eldest child' certainly, but it can also mean first in authority, superior, pre-eminent, the best. That is the meaning that Paul wants us to understand here.

'Father' and 'son' are not just two convenient words to help us to understand the relationship between two persons in the Godhead. The words express a real truth. But that truth is much wider than our limited idea of human parenthood. A human male may become a husband at a point in time and a father at a subsequent time. But God and his Son had no beginning; they were outside time itself and have been described as 'co-eternal'. In any case, God does not have a wife!

Jesus Christ is the one who reconciles all creation to God (verses 18–20)

Paul does not want to provide us with fuel for endless theoretical debates about time and timelessness, or about the complications of the doctrine of the Trinity. He is anxious to emphasize that the Jesus who died on the cross to redeem us was in fact God. 'God was pleased to have all his fulness dwell in him'(verse 19; see overleaf). Jesus is unique. He alone could reconcile heaven and earth. And Paul would surely approve of John Bunyan's bringing all this mind-boggling teaching down to personal experience. In his book *Grace Abounding to the Chief of Sinners* (1666), Bunyan wrote:

> I remember that one day, as I was travelling into the country and musing on the wickedness and blasphemy of my heart, and considering of the enmity that was in me to God, that scripture came into my mind, – 'he hath made peace through the blood of his cross' (Col. 1:20). By which I was made to see, both again, and again and again, that day, that God and my soul were friends by his blood; yea, I saw that the justice of God and my sinful soul could embrace and kiss each other through this blood. This was a good day to me; I hope I shall not forget it (paragraph 115; Everyman edition, page 37).

Questions

1. Some people believe that Jesus was no more than a divinely inspired human being. If this were so, what

would his crucifixion have achieved? What difference does it make if we believe that 'God was in Christ, reconciling the world to himself'? (2 Corinthians 5:19, New Revised Standard Version margin, mirroring this passage).
2. How much does it matter to most of your church members whether Jesus has always existed without a beginning? What difference does it make to our faith?
3. If Jesus Christ is totally pre-eminent, why is the world in such a mess?

Fullness

'Fullness' is one of the key words in Colossians. In the world of commerce it was the word used for the full complement on a ship. The captain would assure himself that all the stores and cargo were on board and correctly stowed, every crew member present and correct, the ship seaworthy and the rigging and sails fully prepared. Then the ship was 'full', ready to go. Nothing more was needed.

It seems that the false teachers in Colosse were trying to persuade the Christians that they lacked fullness, that they were only second-rate believers until they had achieved some sort of extra enlightenment. Paul meets this argument before it appears by pointing out that we already have all the fullness we need if we belong to Jesus Christ. God was pleased to express all his fullness in Christ. All that was necessary to be truly divine is to be found in this Jesus. He was not just one more tinpot deity of the ancient world. All the fullness of God dwells in him. So if we have Jesus Christ we have God. No extra fullness is required. This does not, of course, mean that we cannot or should not grow in our faith; but our ongoing maturity is to be found in Christ, who can give us everything that we need, not in 'Christ-plus-something-more'.

Colossians 1:21–23

The wonder of salvation

Paul spells out very clearly the past plight, present joy and future hope of all true believers.

Paul now gets very excited about what this supreme Christ has done. He is at his bluntest and most direct.

You were enemies (verse 21)

'Your evil behaviour gave you a mindset that was opposed to God,' says Paul in effect. 'You were evil.' No beating about the bush here. It's a relief to find Paul speaking so plainly. Anyone trained in a theological college to be a pastor can say almost anything nicely. The danger is that we allow our niceness to get in the way of the truth; to obscure the reality that without Christ we are evil. We need to face the unwelcome fact that we have done wrong and that doing wrong has warped our minds. Sometimes we want to go on doing wrong. It is a slippery slope.

But you are reconciled (verse 22)

Despite our tendency to slope off in the opposite direction, Christ, the author and sustainer of the universe, has caught up with us and brought about a reconciliation. Now this is not a vague spiritual thing: it is not just symbolism. No, it all happened, through Christ's physical body. This reconciliation came about through something bloody, earthy and solid. The real body of Jesus was attached with real iron nails to a real wooden cross. This is not a philosophical ideal. Jesus was nailed to that cross so that we, with all our sin, could be 'presented without blemish'. This refers to the Old Testament sacrificial system, when a perfect lamb had to be sacrificed to God. Jesus was that perfect Lamb of God, sacrificed on our behalf, so that we could come into God's presence, made holy.

And 'free from accusation'. What a relief it is to us, as it was to the believers in Colosse, that we can be free from accusation! The devil constantly accuses us like this: 'You're not good enough. You have failed before and you will certainly fail again. You feel safe, worshipping in church. You feel good about your faith there. But don't forget that you've got to go home, and then all your good feelings will evaporate and you will fail again.' The great accuser comes to us constantly, but we needn't listen. We can be free from his accusation because Jesus has won that victory. We should remember that victory, with a thrill of joy, when we hear the accusations coming through.

And you will stand firm (verse 23)

This reconciliation and the sense of relief from a nagging false conscience can be ours *if* – if we continue in our faith, established and firm, not moved from the hope held out to us by the gospel. The picture here is of a building, erected firmly on its foundations. The firm foundation is the gospel, and Paul takes us back to the beginning of the letter: 'Do you remember that I am the accredited messenger of the good news from God? That's how firm your foundation is. It is the same gospel that has been published all over the world. And I, Paul, am not only the bearer of the message, but its servant too. I proclaim it and I also sit under its authority.' It is a humble apostle who readily admits that he is no different from his readers in needing the reconciliation that Jesus has promised and which he, Paul, proclaims with such excitement.

Questions

1. 'Your evil behaviour' (verse 21). Deep down we may feel that this evil is exaggerated in our case. In what sense are we all evil and alienated from God? Is there good in each of us too? How do good and evil affect us, before and after our committal to Christ?
2. Do preachers need to persuade unbelievers that they are evil before they can accept the solution to their problem? Can one be a Christian without first having a sense of sin? Share your own and other people's experiences.
3. 'The gospel … that has been proclaimed to every creature under heaven' (verse 23). Has it? What does Paul mean? Perhaps Romans 1:18–20 and Matthew 28:18–20 will help.

Colossians 1:24–29

The task of ministry

The purpose of ministry is both mission and maturity.

 'I fill up in my flesh what is still lacking' (verse 24) does not mean that Christ's suffering was somehow inadequate and that Paul needs to complete it. Christ's suffering had a purpose, and until that purpose is fulfilled something further needs to be done. It is not that Christ has to suffer yet more – his suffering is already sufficient to save the world – but that we need to act in response to it. So Paul works it out in his situation, and takes his part in the suffering of Christ. In the same way all of us need to convey, as it were, the suffering and therefore the blessing,

so that they can be experienced by the people we are in touch with. Then Paul goes on to explain that he has been entrusted with a secret.

The mystery revealed (verses 26–27)

This secret, this mystery, had been hidden from the little market town of Colosse for generations, but now, at last, the plan was revealed; to bring Jesus to the world and the world to Jesus.

Sometimes we have to confess to a childlike pleasure in having a secret. *We* know something *they* don't know. Our church services must look rather like that. It really is quite a bizarre form of behaviour: meeting in a huddle, singing strange songs and talking to an invisible God, while the rest of the world goes on doing its merry things. They don't know why we do it, so what we do must look very odd. But the secret Paul has in mind is an open one. It is intended for everyone, and it is up to him and to us to make it known. We meet in the place of worship in order to go out and tell the mystery of God's glorious news. Why glorious? It doesn't appear so to many of our contemporaries, or even to some of those who worship with us. The answer is: 'Christ in you, the hope of glory' (verse 27). Jesus is in us, his power resides in us, his love is in us. What better hope for the future could we really imagine?

The mission announced (verses 28–29)

Paul was sometimes very blunt, as we have seen already. He admonishes, he teaches, informs and educates, so that everyone present may grow and become mature in the faith. Perhaps we too need to be more direct sometimes in encouraging one another towards a more mature faith. One of the biggest handicaps that the church has to put up with is the immaturity of the people of God. We may be physically fit, highly intelligent and very successful people, but in our faith we blunder about and fail to live as Christ has called us to. Then outsiders look at the church and say, 'Well, if that's what you're like, how can we believe this glorious message you're trying to tell us about? Pull the other one!'

That is why maturity and mission must go hand in hand. 'To this end', says Paul, 'I labour, struggling [literally the word is 'agonizing'] with all his energy, which so powerfully works in me.' Paul works, but God is actually working in him. This is the secret of success for every Christian worker. We work, and God works in and through us. If we work in our own strength we shall find ourselves powerless and ineffective. So mission and the ministry of maturity happen only when we have Christ in us, recognize that we have Christ in us and allow him to do what he wants to do through us.

Questions

1. If Christ has suffered all that is necessary, why should we need to suffer further? Is there any way in which we can suffer on behalf of other people?
2. What do you understand by the phrase 'the mystery of the gospel'? What is mysterious about it? How can we make it plain to people who cannot understand it at all?
3. Do our lives shout so loudly that people cannot hear what the church is saying? Of course, we need to be very careful about our behaviour. But is it better to be open about our shortcomings (for instance, when there is a sexual scandal) or to try to hide them from the public gaze? How should we steer between dishonesty and hypocrisy?

The mystery of the gospel

It seems odd to talk about the crystal-clear good news of the gospel as a 'mystery'. The Greek word *mysterion* means anything hidden or secret, but it was also used in the plural, 'the mysteries', to refer to the sacred rites of the Greek mystery religions in which only those who were initiated could share. Paul often uses the word 'mystery' in his letters, probably because he wants to make plain a contrast between the self-absorbed practices of the cults with their strange rites and cloak-and-dagger secrecy, and the open proclamation of the Christian faith, which is meant not for the few but for everyone. These cultic ideas and practices were at the heart of the false teaching that was preying on the Colossian church, so the 'open secret' would have had a special meaning for them.

It is also plain that to the unbeliever the 'good news' appears to be a complete mystery, in the ordinary sense of a puzzle that seems to have no solution. Paul has written at length about this in the first two chapters of his first letter to the church in Corinth. Only the Holy Spirit can break in to enlighten anyone who cannot see the truth.

We might also note that in medieval times the trade and craft guilds were called 'mysteries'. If you asked a person what his mystery was, you were asking him what his profession was. So the medieval 'mystery plays' were not murder mysteries, but plays performed by the trade or craft guilds. They told the story of creation, sin, judgment and salvation.

DO NOT BE LED ASTRAY FROM CHRIST

Colossians 2

Colossians 2:1–5

The purpose of Paul's ministry:
a strong church

Paul longs for God's people to be able to see the truths of Christ clearly and to avoid seductive errors.

For our own convenience we have called this 'Part 2', and the Bible begins a new chapter; but there were no chapter divisions in Paul's original letter. They were added much later. The apostle in fact continues without a break from what we call Colossians 1:29 to 2:1: 'God is working powerfully in me and I can tell you that I am finding it a struggle,' he says in effect.

Paul's agony of spirit (verse 1)

Paul had never met the Christians in Colosse or Laodicea face to face, but again he says that he was struggling or agonizing over them. Paul's gifts were not confined to theology and church-planting. He had a pastoral, loving heart even for people he had never met. That same Paul, under the inspiration of the Holy Spirit, reaches out across two thousand years and has compassion for us as people he has not yet seen. His writing touches our hearts as it did those who first read this letter in Colosse. It is a pattern for all who are entrusted with pastoral care or ministry in the church. We are called to care, not in a casual way, or as a means to earn a living, but with agony of soul for the sheep in our flock.

Unity and love in Christ (verses 2–3)

Paul's purpose is not to tear down but to build up. He is about to confront his readers with some strong words, but his purpose is that they should be united in love. These are not empty phrases. The young church was in acute danger from false teachers. The effect of false teaching is never unity and love but invariably disunity, factions, splinter groups and sects, and consequently suspicion, animosity, even hatred. When false teaching comes in, unity and love go out of the window.

In verse 2 Paul writes of the 'full riches' of the 'mystery of God', namely Christ. The false teachers were apparently urging that Christians need more than Christ, a greater fullness that comes from a mystical experience to which they alone held the key. Jesus on his own was not enough. 'But', Paul is saying, 'Jesus is enough. There can be no greater fullness than the fullness of this wonderful Son of God.' Yet the Christian mind should never be complacent. None of us has grasped all the biblical truths we are ever going to need. We are all students, disciples, till the day we die, learning and enriching our knowledge of God so that we can be protected from Satan's entanglements.

This is Paul's major argument; all the treasures of wisdom and knowledge are to be found in Christ, not somewhere beyond him. It is in Christ that everything happens. We need never be ashamed to focus simply on Jesus Christ. He is, after all, the Lord of the universe. He is both simple ('gentle Jesus, meek and mild') and profound (the source of every aspect of wisdom and knowledge. See also 'The mystery of the gospel' on page 42).

Do not be deceived (verses 4–5)

'I tell you this', says Paul, 'so that no-one may deceive you with fine-sounding arguments.' If we possess the wisdom to be found in Christ, we shall be able to spot heretical, false teaching at a hundred paces. That is why immature

45

Christians and backslidden Christians are the most vulnerable to the cults. The immature may be full of warmth and enthusiasm but may lack knowledge, and so be unable to spot the false teaching for what it is. The backslidden may be well educated in the things of God, but may have forgotten a great deal, have grown cold, and may not even want to avoid error – they may even find it attractive and exciting. So we need to grow in maturity and in love for Christ and for one another, if we are to be safe from the advance of erroneous teaching.

Questions

1. Doctors and social workers are advised not to become emotionally involved with their patients or clients because the strain would drain and exhaust them. How then should Christian leaders follow Paul's example of agonizing over his flock, even those he had never seen, without collapsing under the burden?
2. How can you 'spot heretical teaching at a hundred paces'? How do you set about evaluating the riches of new wisdom that come to you through books or preachers? How can you tell the true from the false?
3. Worldwide and across denominations, churches are not united, yet most claim that we share a basic unity. Which divisions should we be concerned about, and which are to be accepted as unimportant? What is that basic unity?

'The heart'

Paul wants his readers to be encouraged 'in heart' (verse 2). The New Testament does not mean exactly what we do when we use the word 'heart'. We tend to think of emotional warmth; 'affairs of the heart' are romantic. But Paul means much more than that. He includes the mind too, and means the very core or centre of human experience. The heart, in this sense, is of course a symbol or metaphor. Literally, the heart is an organ that gets the blood round the body. We never intend to suggest that we love someone with all our blood-pump! The Jews located what we call the heart, in the emotional sense, in the bowels. The old King James Bible spoke of 'bowels of mercy'. Imagine a first-century Jewish boy telling his girlfriend, 'I love you with all my bowels.' It lacks a certain romantic flavour!

Paul is concerned neither with blood-pumps nor with the digestive system; neither with raw emotion nor even with a 'feel-good factor'. He is concerned with thoughtful faith, thoroughly tested by experience; encouragement at our core, which keeps us going on and going on; the full riches of unity in Christ.

'Present with you in spirit'

'I am absent from you in body,' says Paul, 'but present with you in spirit' (verse 5). This is one of the phrases that Christians sometimes use as a cop-out. 'I can't come to the meeting tonight but I'll be with you in spirit.' Some speakers have to address a very few bodies and a large company of spirits! 'With you in spirit' does not mean, 'I'd rather watch the football on TV.' It reflects the pastoral heart of verse 1: Paul is really struggling on behalf of these people. He is in prison in Rome, yet he is still agonizing for the Laodiceans and Colossians, whom he has never met. 'In my agony of soul', he implies, 'I delight to see how orderly you are.' Maybe he had in mind a picture of ranks and ranks of Roman soldiers lined up; no-one could fail to be impressed by how orderly, how mature, how firm, how strong they were. The faith of the Colossian believers was very firm indeed. It needed to be, because they were being attacked at that very moment. They needed the presence of Paul's spirit, struggling on their behalf in the spiritual battle.

Colossians 2:6–12

The battle between empty false teaching and fullness in Christ

---

Christ provides for all our needs for spiritual maturity. To demand 'Christ-and-something-more' is dangerous.

Paul has laid the foundations for his appeal to his readers: their faithfulness, the supremacy of Christ, and the purpose of ministry (to grow mature disciples). Now he is ready to confront the false teaching endangering the church. He gives the Colossians a 'do' and a 'don't'. Do continue down the right road. Conversely, don't wander off the beaten track.

Continue down the right road (verses 6–7)

'Just as you received Christ Jesus as Lord' (note the emphasis on his authority, his lordship), 'continue to live in him.' The false teachers were arguing that there was one way perhaps to find faith – Jesus is enough for your initial salvation – but when it comes to maturity, finding the fullness of God, there was a new and better way which they could offer. It looks as if there were certain Jewish rituals involved in the attainment of this higher knowledge they claimed to offer. But Paul affirms very clearly that, just as Jesus was quite enough for initial salvation (a point conceded by the false teachers), so he is equally sufficient for all that we need for the future.

This teaching from Paul is very important for us in the twenty-first century. We are all in danger of getting into a rut, getting stuck at a certain point in our faith; and we look around for a way forward, to give us a new sense of power and authority. Of course we all need the Holy Spirit to give us experience of the love and power of Jesus. But the Holy Spirit does not lead us on and *away* from Jesus Christ, but more deeply *into* him. We need to be very careful that we grow in Christ: to depart from him is not to grow but to shrivel. If we remain rooted in Christ where we started, then we can grow freely and with overflowing thankfulness. The tragedy in many of our churches is our lack of thankfulness. There is no attitude of gratitude. Paul wants nothing of a dry doctrine that makes people miserable. To hold on to Christ is to hold the real truth, and it results in a wonderful, heartfelt gratitude, overflowing with thankfulness.

Don't wander off the beaten track (verse 8)

'See to it' is a throat-grabbing little phrase that implies, 'Wake up!' 'Get a grip!' 'Watch out!' This teaching they were hearing looked so full, so exciting. All these heady ideas about myriads of angels who whirl about God, all these mysterious and weird observances, looked incredibly deep. Compared with the simple old gospel, they were very attractive, yet opened up they were empty. How disappointing it is for a child to receive a large, beautifully wrapped present, only to discover something inside that is boring and unwanted! These Colossian converts were coming with wide-eyed innocence to the tinsel and trappings of an intriguing philosophy. 'But', Paul implies, 'it will prove to be a huge disappointment to you. The package is empty.'

Live fully in Christ (verses 9–10)

All the fullness of God dwells in Christ in bodily form

(summing up 1:15–20), which is why we need only Christ for a full life. Jesus is all that is necessary of God for us, completely God. Amazingly, we have fullness in Christ; all the information we need to live a full life, and all the experience we need, too. We need not be afraid of this fullness. Thousands of Christians have settled for forgiveness, and that's great, but that's all. They have no overwhelming sense of gratitude; they lack the fullness of Jesus. May the Lord deliver us from a faith in which there is no power or passion, no victory over all that drags us down. There are many 'elemental forces' ranging the world, but Jesus is more than equal to them all. And he came so that we might live life to the full.

Say goodbye to your old, flawed nature (verses 11–12)

Why does Paul suddenly mention circumcision here? It may be because the false teachers were emphasizing the need for rituals, perhaps including circumcision, and legalistic obedience to certain set rules. Paul reminds us that what matters is not so much circumcision done with a knife, but that cutting-out of evil from the heart which can be done only by Christ himself. In fact, many non-Jews were coming to Christian faith and were not bothered about the Jewish rite of circumcision. The critical factor, as Paul saw it, was that we are 'buried with him [Christ] in baptism', that symbolic act in which we are 'drowned' but come back to new life. There is no need for us to argue about how much water is needed to make the symbol effective. The image is where the power lies. We are dead to our old, sinful nature and risen to new life in the power of God.

Questions

1. 'Spirit baptism' is a common experience among Christians today. Some have argued that this is just the kind of thing that Paul was warning his readers against,

because it leads us away from Christ in favour of the Holy Spirit. How do you respond to this opinion?
2. Let each member of the group make a list of the kind of dangerous new ideas which might lead Christians off the beaten track today. After an agreed time, compare and discuss your lists.
3. Why did Jesus add to his command to make disciples the words 'baptising them in the name of the Father and of the Son and of the Holy Spirit' (Matthew 28:19)?

Subtle deceptions

'Human tradition and the basic principles of this world.' This phrase from verse 8 is difficult to understand. Paul is describing things diametrically opposed to Christ, a hollow and deceptive philosophy that takes people captive instead of granting them the freedom that Jesus had promised: 'you will know the truth, and the truth will set you free' (John 8:32).

The 'basic principles' may refer to the ABC of knowledge; the simple, obvious truths of everyday life. Paul may have been saying, in effect, 'You think this new teaching is incredibly profound and exciting, but I assure you it's all just common sense dressed up. Don't go back to that old-hat stuff when you could be enjoying new life in Christ'.

But Paul may also be referring to the Old Testament law, which we are judged by and which we can never measure up to. He uses exactly this phrase 'basic principles' when discussing slavery under the law and our new freedom in Christ, in Galatians 4:3.

v. 8.

The New Revised Standard Version of the Bible translates this difficult phrase, 'the elemental spirits of the universe'. This gives us a clue to another possible meaning Paul may have had in mind: 'Do not return to a pagan approach to life, bound by fear of evil spirits and superstitious rituals, which are intended to protect you from them.'

Whatever Paul means exactly, it is clear that we should be growing up in Christ, freed from the shackles of traditional deceptions.

Colossians 2:13–15

Three enemies defeated

Jesus has already defeated sin, the dictates of the law and the power of evil. There is no need for us to waver and fall back into slavery to these things.

Paul is anxious to remind his readers from what kind of life they have been rescued. He seems to be afraid that they are on the brink of snatching defeat from the very jaws of victory. Having been freed from sin, the ceremonial law and Satan, they seem to be on the edge of collapsing into heresy and spiritual slavery. So Paul reminds them very vividly of the three powerful enemies already defeated for them by Jesus. The new Christians have been raised to new life from the deadness of sin, freed from the dead hand of a code of regulations and saved from the deadly power of evil.

Raised to new life from the deadness of sin (verse 13)

For many of us 'new life' might sound like an exaggeration. As the years go by, we may get used to the idea of Christ's benefits in giving us new life and tend to view our past through rose-tinted spectacles. Paul had no such illusions. We used to be dead in trespasses and sins; we were not alive at all. Becoming a Christian was not simply a patch-up job but the raising to life of that which was dead. Only Jesus is able to do that. The enemy, sin, was clearly defeated at that first Easter when Jesus leapt out of the tomb. That is a fact of history which cannot now be reversed, because it happened. That past fact has made it possible for us, in the present, to be made alive in him. Jesus, at the cross, forgave all our sins, every one of them.

Freed from the dead hand of a code of regulations (verse 14)

What is this 'written code' and what are these 'regulations'? Surely they have nothing to do with us in the twenty-first century? The reference is to the Jewish law, the 'Torah', the first five books of the Old Testament, but elaborated into hundreds of do's and don'ts that strict Jews tried to obey. God had never said that the law would save people, even if they could obey all of it; but there was a popular view that it would. This led to the iron grip of guilt on everyone, because however hard they tried to keep the law, they always failed somewhere along the line. It is a sad fact that, after two thousand 'years of grace', the good news that we no longer have to struggle to reach a standard of goodness before God will accept us has still not penetrated far into human understanding. Even churchgoers, even committed Christians, often feel, deep down, that they have hoops to jump through, obstacles to leap over, meetings and services to attend and good works to perform, to induce God to love and accept them.

Paul utters a resounding 'no' to all of this. It has all been cancelled and nailed to the cross. He may be referring to a charge-sheet, a written list of the crimes of a convicted criminal. It has been taken, crossed through and nailed to the cross of Jesus, where he will now take all responsibility for it. The criminal goes free. Some of us may look back to a betrayal in our marriage, years ago, and live with the guilt of it still. Some of us have lived with the consequences of a lie or a deceit. The list could be endless. But Jesus calls us to come to him and have our list nailed to the cross. It has all been cancelled. That is what Christian forgiveness is all about: the demands of the written code cancelled and a new start made with a clean sheet of paper.

Saved from the deadly power of evil (verse 15)

Jesus has defeated sin and the law, and has defeated the evil 'powers and authorities' too. He has made a 'public spectacle' of them. In the world of Paul's day, a Roman conqueror would bring back to Rome a line of bedraggled troops, hostages, slaves and valuable goods from a defeated country – sometimes even its king. Forced to walk, chained, in the victory parade, they would be ridiculed and mocked. The power of Satan and his evil forces may have seemed overwhelming, but now Christ has made a mockery of them. He had disarmed them and shown them to the world as having no more power to harm us.

'Sin and law and Satan have all been defeated,' says Paul in effect, 'so there's no need to fall back into any of these prison cells from which you have been freed.' He gives examples of what he means in the next few verses.

Questions

1. In your group compare notes, where appropriate, about how you view your past. Were you 'dead in your sins'? Not everyone can pin down a time when they made a profession of faith. Can one become a Christian gradually? (Be tactful and prepare to be helpful towards any who are unsure whether they are Christians or not.)
2. In what ways are Christians tempted to behave as if they had to justify themselves and reach a high moral standard in order to be acceptable to God? Why does this feeling subtly intrude itself even when we understand the meaning of undeserved grace?
3. How can you help a person who says, 'Yes, I know that

God has forgiven my sins, but I cannot feel that he has. I still feel guilty'? Some members of the group may well admit to these feelings.

Confronting error

In this section of his letter, Paul has been very direct – quite aggressive, in fact. As we saw earlier, it is sometimes possible to be so nice that the point we are trying to make is quite lost. We certainly need to treat people with great tact and gentleness, but we may also need to treat error with rigorous clarity. If a person is about to fall over a cliff, we shout first and apologize afterwards! The church can be kept pure under the attacks of false teaching only if we are clear about what is true and are ready to say so.

The Bible is often more blunt than we expect. For instance, Nehemiah was annoyed with the people of God for marrying wives from outside their faith. The Living Bible paraphrase of Nehemiah 13:25 makes plain what happened next: 'I argued with these parents and cursed them and punched a few of them and knocked them around and pulled out their hair; and they vowed before God that they would not let their children intermarry with non-Jews.'

You bet they did! This, we must emphasize, illustrates how urgently Nehemiah felt the need to set these people straight; it is definitely not an example to us of how to treat people we don't agree with! The Nehemiahs among us need to learn to unclench their fists, but none of us should remain permanently silent when we see our brothers or sisters in Christ heading into spiritual danger.

Colossians 2:16–23

Three impostors exposed

In following Christ we need to take care not to become enslaved to human observances, fashionable experiences or petty rules and regulations.

Secure as we are, then, on the foundations that Jesus Christ has laid for us, what have we to fear? Come on, Paul, why are you so worried about these Colossian Christians? The problem for them, and perhaps for us too, is that Satan has many disguises. If he cannot prevent us from being Christians, he can distort our view of what Christianity is. Then he can head us away from the truth into what seems to be an ever more religious life. So Paul warns us all against overemphasis on religious observances, religious experiences and religious rules.

Religious observances (verses 16–17)

Having religious scruples about certain foods, new-moon celebrations and special Sabbath days looks like a mixture of heresies, mostly Jewish in origin. Doing all the right things and avoiding all the wrong things on certain days might well divert our attention from Christ. These young Christians were probably being told that the new moon, their star sign and the movement of the planets affected the way they lived. This letter reads almost like a modern newspaper. Horoscopes were alive and well in the first century just as they are in the twenty-first. If the 'Your Life in the Stars' column tells you that Thursday is a good day for business deals, do we not have a lurking suspicion that there may be something in it? All these things, says Paul, are only a shadow. Many Christians today have lived for so long in the shadowy half-light that we would hardly recognize the light if we saw it. We see the central issues of the gospel very dimly. But it is Jesus, not religious observances, who will save us. They will not disciple us. They will not mature us.

Some Christians value religious observances more than others do, but most of us have our weaknesses in this direction. We have a whole range of habits, certain kinds of behaviour, ways of dress even, that are more important to us than we like to admit – and woe betide anyone who disagrees with them! We often judge people on the basis of their observances. We may see people worshipping with arms raised and eyes closed, for example. Depending on our own point of view, we may say, 'They must be really spiritual', or 'Look at them, parading their mock piety.' What do we think about people who worship with their hands in their pockets? It is easy to be drawn into making judgments on the basis of such trivial matters, though to some they are not trivial. The Tempter will always be pleased if he can get us to add something to a simple faith in Christ. He is glad if we do things in a particular way so that we can delude ourselves into thinking we are being specially godly. Don't listen to him.

Religious experiences (verses 18–19)

Another ever-present danger for Christians is to suppose that religious experiences are the proof of religious reality. All such experiences must be brought to the touchstone of the Word of God, evaluated by the Scriptures and laid at the feet of Jesus. This does not mean that we don't need religious experiences or should try to avoid them, but they are not to be seen as a measure of our maturity. The ecstatic worship of angels, detailed visions of glory or overwhelming feelings of humility may transport us into another realm emotionally, but what matters is whether they transform our lives. If these experiences are not centred on Christ, they won't. There is a huge difference between transportation and transformation.

A preacher's illustration may help to sharpen the point. A farmer and his family visited the Big City for the first time in their lives and stayed in a hotel. They had never seen an escalator or lift before. What was the cupboard inside the sliding door for? An old lady with a walking-stick went inside, and the door closed. A few moments later, the door opened and a very attractive young woman stepped out. The farmer turned to his son and said, 'Quick! Go and fetch your mother!' Transportation and transformation are not the same thing.

Religious rules (verses 20–23)

'Don't do this! Don't do that! Don't do the other thing!' That is not what the good news of the gospel is all about. We have been rescued from that sort of thing. Paul's argument goes something like this: 'Don't get drawn back into keeping petty rules and regulations to be thought especially holy or wise. You're dead to all that, remember? These rules are devised by human beings, not by God. They may well give the appearance of wisdom. Harsh treatment of the body to make you more holy is what some people tell you that you need. But it is not what God wants. Oh, and by the way, it doesn't work. These do's and don'ts 'lack any value in restraining sensual indulgence'. The cold shower may give you a smug sense of achievement (if it doesn't give you a heart attack!) but it will not make you a better person.

In his forthright attack on false teaching Paul has made a powerful point: religious rules, observances and experiences are dangerous if we believe they can lead to a higher life than Christ can give us. This does not mean they are all to be avoided, however. We shall explore this further in the questions that follow.

Questions

1. 'Do this in remembrance of me,' said Jesus. The Communion Service or Lord's Supper is a religious observance, rightly treasured by God's people and commanded by Jesus himself. How is it different from the observances that Paul is warning us about? In what ways might the Lord's Supper itself lead us away from Christ?
2. Share some religious experiences in your group. Be careful not to judge one another. In general, which kinds of experience are helpful and which unhelpful? Why? How far does the answer depend on the individual's personality?
3. If we abandon all the rules, how can we know whether we are doing right or wrong? Does Paul mean that we are not to submit to the Ten Commandments? How can we decide which rules to obey and which to ignore?

Fasting

Paul warns us against thinking that mistreating our bodies can result in a growth in holiness. Yet in his first letter to the Corinthians (9:24–27) he recommends strict training, and actually says, 'I beat my body and make it my slave so that after I have preached to others, I myself will not be disqualified for the prize.' How can we understand this? And where does fasting from food or drink come in? Jesus fasted. It can't be wrong for us, surely?

Yes, it can be. It depends on our motives and the way we set about it. If we go without food because we think God will therefore automatically be pleased with us and that we shall earn his favour and his blessing, we have totally misunderstood the freedom of the gospel.

But if we fast in obedience to Scripture or to express our

seriousness about a particular issue, that's great. We may need to abstain from the usual pattern of our life in order to concentrate for a time on prayer. That's great. Some Christians use Lent, the forty days before Easter, to give time to reflection, study or devotion. That's great. Fasting can be of great value if entered into humbly, with the advice and support of fellow-Christians and with the aim of drawing closer to Christ, but it is not a means of earning merit.

LIVE HOLY LIVES
IN CHRIST

Colossians 3:1 – 4:1

Colossians 3:1–4

The battle for the mind

The sure foundation for right belief and action is Christ. We need to decide to set our sights clearly on him.

There is rather a jolt at the end of chapter 2. Chapter 3 doesn't seem to follow on logically. So we must stand back and look again at the shape of the whole let-
ter. Paul has emphasized the uniqueness of Christ as the Son of God and the only way to God. The Colossians had accepted this salvation, but were in grave danger of cutting off the very branch they were sitting on by buying into the weird, sectarian views of the false teachers.

The story is told of a barracks in the west of England where a large, metal box was found outside the gate. Fearing terrorists, a bomb-disposal unit carried out a controlled explosion, releasing a cascade of scraps of paper. On examination, these were found to be thousands of leaflets, describing how to deal with suspicious-looking boxes. They had destroyed the very thing that was designed to help them.

At a much more serious level, this is what the Colossians were in danger of doing.

Focus your mind on what Christ has done (verses 1–2)

Now we are ready to see where Paul's thoughts are leading us. He seems quite deliberately to be saying this: If you want to avoid the false teaching that demands all kinds of religious observances, rules and experiences in addition to your faith in Jesus, you will have to focus on him, think about him and understand all that the cross alone has accomplished. But you will also need to live the right kind of lifestyle. A decision has to be made: whether to stay true to Christ in devotion and action, or to follow the 'new' teaching. This decision has to be made in the heart (verse 1) and the mind (verse 2). As we have seen (page 46), the 'heart' in the New Testament is the core of our being, the ultimate decision-making function. This involves both your commitment of faith and the way you behave. The focus of both is 'the things above, where Christ is seated at the right hand of God' (verse 1).

Verse 2 is very Jewish in style. It parallels and more or less repeats verse 1. This literary device occurs frequently in the Psalms (for instance, Psalm 34:1: 'I will extol the LORD at all times; his praise will always be on my lips'). Paul is using this repetition to emphasize his point. We are raised with Christ; that is our position theologically. So we should let our minds dwell on that fact, so that our behaviour will begin to mirror in practice what is true already in spirit. We are seated with Christ in the heavenly places. So we must now set our minds on becoming what we are. This demands a certain focus, a seriousness of commitment. Many Christians slide away from orthodox belief simply because their minds have wandered off on to other things. Satan is constantly on the watch for wandering minds. We need to be absorbed with Christ.

Focus your mind on what Christ will do (verses 3–4)

At first sight the idea of being dead to the old way of life looks like a matter of great self-sacrifice, as if we are turning our backs on the good world around us and on all the good things we used to enjoy. But Paul wants us to look forward to something much better. When Christ, who is our life, appears, we shall appear with him in glory. Some old versions of verse 4 do have 'our' instead of 'your'. That would suggest that Paul was saying, 'I'm not just preaching at you; we're all in this together.'

We need to adopt a 'glory perspective' here. We are meant to behave ourselves properly, not because some puritanical god is glaring down at us, ready to wag his finger at us when we go wrong, but because glory awaits us. Our obedience now is a mere foretaste of the purity and perfection that will be ours in Christ. Christians live better in the present when they feel sure of their destiny hereafter. It is sometimes hard for us to believe in that destiny, because we see moral failure on every side and we fear that the church is about to be engulfed. Yet glory awaits us, and we need to struggle to keep our eyes focused on Christ.

Questions

1. Try to explain, as if to a person who knows nothing about Christianity, what being 'raised with Christ' means to you. If you feel strong enough in your group, try a role play.
2. Our beliefs affect our behaviour, and our behaviour affects our beliefs. Read 'Manipulating your beliefs' below, and discuss how far you agree with these statements.
3. How sure are you that you never manipulate your beliefs to justify your actions? Perhaps you can discuss this in your group – but take care not to accuse one another.
4. How can we be more aware of being 'dead to the old life' and looking forward to glory in the new? Be practical, and give examples of what this means.

Manipulating your beliefs

Many of us would agree that our beliefs affect our actions, but few of us realize that the way we behave ultimately changes the way we think and believe. For instance, someone may be clear that adultery is wrong; there's no doubt about that. Yet that person may fall into an intense sexual relationship with someone else's wife or husband, may walk out on his or her own marriage, and then attempt to justify that action morally – and even biblically. This has happened to Christian leaders with very sound, orthodox beliefs. Yet when their behaviour failed to match their beliefs, they have attempted to manipulate their beliefs to fit their actions. This may seem incredible to us. Certainly we do not want to believe it, yet it happens all too often. We should be slow to condemn and quick to pray for people in this sort of dilemma.

Paul wants us to see that if we persist in behaving in an ungodly way, our belief-system will decay. If we move away from God in terms of behaviour, our faith in God will become increasingly fragile. There is a bridge between faith and practice, and the traffic moves both ways. The strength of our faith helps us to live well; the upright life undergirds the assurance of our faith.

Martin Luther and the Protestant Reformation taught us that salvation is by faith alone, not by good works. Too much emphasis on this undoubted truth may leave us unprotected when we are tempted to immoral behaviour. Good works and wholesome moral living will not save us, but they matter very much.

Colossians 3:5–7

Killing off the old life

We need to turn away from wrongdoing, and also from wrong ideas about what wrongdoing is.

If we are to focus on Christ – Christ incarnate, Christ glorified – rather than on the dazzling array of angelic beings (or whatever takes their place for us today), something has to happen to us. We have to put to death our former life, to kill off that earthly nature that was opposed to God and to go on killing it off continually. It's a hard saying, but Paul is very direct, impolite and blunt. We must leave that old nature no room to wriggle off the hook. So we need to be practical. What does this mean to us in our everyday life?

Sexual relationships

Paul lists the things that belong to our 'earthly' nature:

▶ *Sexual immorality*. The Greek word *porneia* is a catch-all term for almost any kind of sexual impurity.

▶ *Impurity* – just in case we haven't got the message.

▶ *Lust*.

▶ *Evil desires*.

▶ *Greed, which is idolatry*. This is the only item on the list that is not obviously linked with the sexual appetite, and many writers have assumed that it means greed for sexual experience, to such an extent that it becomes an object of worship.

At this point our hearts may sink. Here goes Paul again: Paul the woman-hater, Paul the killjoy, always going on about sex. Hasn't the church had enough bad press in this area without bringing it all up again? Surely there are plenty of other sins to worry about! Yes, there are, and half-a-dozen are going to be listed in verses 8–9, but before we dismiss Paul's emphasis as stuffy or unrealistic for the twenty-first century, we should consider two things.

1. If the media are correct (TV, magazines, films, videos, contemporary novels, the internet), sexuality is indeed an object of worship. The impression conveyed is that 'good' or 'fulfilling' sexual experience is the chief purpose of life. In the Greek and Roman world of Paul's time the same

attitude prevailed. It would be very strange to have a discussion on right and wrong while totally ignoring the central preoccupation of the world we live in.

2. The sexual act and sexual feelings do provide a playground for the enemy, Satan, in a unique way, because they have the power to make such a ghastly mess of people's lives. Misuse of sex can ruin one's own sense of worth, relationship with husbands, wives and especially children, with church and society and with God himself. If our sexuality can be corrupted, significant damage can be done to the cause of Christ and God's values in the world. Rightly welcomed and enjoyed, sexuality is one of the sublimest of God's gifts. There is nothing wrong with sex in itself, and everything right. Perhaps precisely because of its wonderful power and ability to give joy, when it is corrupted it can work just as powerfully in the opposite direction.

Paul in context

Before we go any further it would be useful to unpack a little what we said above about attitudes to sex in the world of the first-century Roman Empire. There is currently an odd idea in general circulation that sexual freedom was invented in the 'swinging sixties' of the last century. But the decaying Roman Empire was a legend for sexual excess. Even bestiality was not unknown at the court of the Caesars. Sexual promiscuity was widespread, and this was made worse by two other practices: the almost vicious subjugation of women, who were thus treated as playthings, almost as slaves, with very few rights of their own; and the merging of religious ecstasy with sexual ecstasy. This, in practice, meant the employment, in many ancient religions, of temple prostitutes to satisfy the religious and physical appetites of the 'worshippers'.

Given this background, it is hardly surprising that Paul should want to warn his friends about the dangers of twisted and corrupted sexuality. But, and this was as important for them as it is for us, the Colossians would have grown up in a climate of sexual distortion so that it seemed to them natural and normal. Paul's warnings probably came as a shock. 'Sexual purity.' What could that mean? What is he getting at? What a revolutionary idea!

Where are the guidelines?

Our modern ways of thinking are very much in tune with the values of the ancient world here. Sex is seen largely as fun, the normal fulfilment of our right to express ourselves exactly as we like. Playboys rule OK. In the face of this, the churches have either retreated into prudery or caved in and accepted this state of things as inevitable. In either case, we have nowhere to go for a fully fledged and balanced biblical view of sexuality. It is to the everlasting shame of the leaders of our churches that we have been too embarrassed to give clear and authoritative guidelines about sexuality. There are some notable exceptions to this rule, but on the whole we find a complete generation (or two) of Christians growing up with no grasp of what the right approach to sexuality should be. It has been said that chastity was one of the few brand-new virtues that Christianity brought to the ancient world. The idea that you should, or even could, be chaste before marriage and faithful afterwards is similarly new and astonishing to many people today – even to Christians. At best, it is acknowledged as an ideal, but not one that can be expected to work out in practice.

So the enemy, Satan, is winning an important victory. Not only has he taken something wonderfully good and wholesome and distorted and corrupted it; but he has sold to us, through the media and politically correct liberal thinking, the idea that this distorted version is the natural and normal one. Christians who stand for wholesome, biblical values are either jeered at or ignored, and are not even understood. Others have merely floated with the tide. We are exposed to a huge range of impurity in thought as well as action through the media, especially the internet. These stimuli do not satisfy our urges but promote our greed: we want more and more. At this point, where Christians need most help to come to terms with our glorious sexuality and the ghastly mess that can become of it, we are left with no clear guidelines.

But Satan is not the only player in this drama. These twisted attitudes towards our sexuality are, of course, of deep concern to the Creator. And they attract his wrath (verse 6)! See below for more reflection on this alarming prospect.

Questions

1. Are sexual sins worse than any other kind? If so, why? If not, how can we make it clear that all sin is an extremely serious matter?
2. How do we understand the wrath of God? Is it something we should talk about to unbelievers? How can we help the depressed and those with tender consciences to see beyond God's wrath to his everlasting love?
3. 'The remedy for misuse is not disuse but right use.' How should we welcome and develop our sexuality as church members? How does it affect married people in relation to single? How do we relate to the unmarried who live with partners? Single people are sexual beings just like everyone else. What is 'right use' of sexuality for them?
4. What is the 'right use' of sexuality for homosexual and lesbian Christians? Does it differ from what is right for single heterosexual people?

The wrath of God

The age of the hell-fire sermon, which terrified people into loving God (or so it was assumed), is now past. But at the same time, we seem to have lost a very clear biblical emphasis: God's just, inflexible and passionate hatred of all evil, corruption and vice.

The word 'wrath' carries for many of us the picture of a face distorted with fury, mindlessly punishing the evil-doer. This does not describe the God of love and justice whom we find in the pages of the Bible and in our own experience. God does not lose his temper. But he does hate sin. If we fail to tell people this, we do them a great dis-service and caricature the God of the New Testament as well as of the Old. He is infinitely loving, and his forgive-ness flows in waves from the cross; but he is also absolutely just. He can and will forgive sin, but he cannot pass it by as if it didn't exist. This may be hard for us to understand, but it is biblically true.

Paul tells us that the wrath of God is directed against sexual sin. How then does this tie in with Jesus' treatment of the woman caught in adultery (John 7:53 – 8:1), or his keeping company with prostitutes (Luke 7:39)? It is surely clear that God hates their corrupted ways, but does not hate *them*. Indeed, he loves them so much that they can be forgiven and restored to a wholesome life. Surely the same must be true for us, however far we may have fallen. The wrath of God is directed at the distortion and corruption of his good gifts; in this case, sexuality. If we continue to live by these twisted values, we are in danger of placing ourselves out of the range of his love. He longs to embrace us all, but will not override our determined choice of evil. A solemn thought!

Colossians 3:8–11

The true equality

If we are united in Christ Jesus, the old way of life must perish and false social barriers must be demolished.

At the end of the previous section (verse 7), Paul told us that he had in mind not just improvement in moral behaviour but a new perspective on life itself: we used to look at things one way, but now we see life from a completely new angle. We may be reminded of Jesus' meeting with the 'rich young ruler' (Luke 18:18–22). This man had done well in moral terms' and expected to be told how to do even better. But Jesus cut sharply across his whole way of thinking: 'Sell everything you have and give to the poor.' A radical change of attitude is called for. As before, we need practical examples of what this implies.

More practical guidelines (verses 8–9)

Here then is another list of attitudes and actions that are not acceptable in the new life. This is not because they break religious rules, but because they are opposed to the new relationship of love that Christ has set up for us.

- *Anger and rage;* not an indignant feeling against injustice (sometimes called 'righteous anger'), but smouldering resentment that goes on and on in bitterness, or blazing temper that is out of control.

- *Malice*: this suggests a twisted sneer of the lips as we do someone down.

- *Slander*: untruth about others whom we want to hurt.

▶ *Filthy language*: this includes swearing, blasphemy and the language of the gutter.

▶ *Lying*: this perhaps summarizes the list; saying or being something we are not, presenting an insincere face to others. Satan is the father of lies (John 8:44), and this is just the sort of behaviour that pleases him. Then again comes the reminder that these were examples of the ways of the old life, the old self. The Christian has taken off the old life like a suit of ragged and dirty clothes, and so the habits of the old life (no pun intended, but it makes the point) must stay in the bin where they belong.

Know who your father is (verse 10)

Our new self is constantly being renewed in the knowledge and image of its Creator, God the Father. We are not intended to lie like the father of lies, Satan. We tend to act like our fathers, so we should make sure we know who our father is!

Most people enjoy looking at family photographs, portraits and holiday pictures. It's not long before someone says, 'I can see his father in him, can't you?' or, 'Doesn't she take after her mother?' The odd thing is that the children concerned can very rarely see the likeness that is obvious to others. Perhaps that is as it should be. If our father is our Creator, we should be living so that others can see the family likeness in what we do and say. If we are unconscious of the fact that we are mirroring our Father, so much the better. We shall be free at least from self-righteousness.

All social barriers demolished (verse 11)

This ringing denunciation of the barriers we humans have erected between races, cultures, classes and religious beliefs follows logically from the assertion that God is the Father of us all. If, in our new life, we mirror his life, these petty distinctions will all melt away and we shall be all one in Christ Jesus (Galatians 3:28). But how petty *are* these distinctions, in fact? Pride of race, culture, class or religion runs very powerfully in our veins, and is sometimes seen at its worst in our denominational divisions. There can be an arrogance about our distinctive beliefs that minimizes the role of Jesus and is to our shame. Denominational allegiance is not wrong, but if we elevate our special practices above the unity that we have in Jesus Christ we are in great danger.

The story is told of a Southern Baptist, preaching at a convention in the United States.

'Isn't it good that we are all Baptists here?' he enthused. 'It's a wonderful thing. Is there anyone here who is not a Baptist?'

One little old lady put up her hand.

'Well,' said the preacher, 'and what are you if you're not a Baptist?'

'I'm a Methodist,' she replied.

'And why are you a Methodist?'

'My father was a Methodist and my grandfather was a Methodist.'

'So *that's* why you're a Methodist!' exclaimed the preacher, warming to his task. 'What if your father had been an idiot and your grandfather had been an idiot?' (Laughter.)

'Well,' she ventured, 'I guess I'd have been a Baptist.'

(Any Southern Baptists reading this story will no doubt, of their generosity, forgive us for retelling it. It could have happened to anyone!)

There is no room for an allegiance higher than to Christ. That was revolutionary stuff in the first century, and it is just as revolutionary now. And it brings us back full circle to Paul's concern to eliminate the false teaching. Some believers claimed to have special insights and to be holier than others. No, we are all equal before God, for 'Christ is all, and is in all'.

Questions

1. Individual stocktaking. Look carefully, prayerfully and honestly at the list of examples of 'old-life' behaviour in verses 8–9. How far does each one still apply to you? Pray for help.
2. Together, make a list of your denominational or fellowship distinctives. What makes you different from other Christian groupings? Which distinctive is most important to you? How important is it really?
3. What social barriers exist in your neighbourhood (see verse 11)? How can they be broken down? Is this a political question or a Christian concern? How can Christians help to encourage excellence and at the same time demonstrate equality?

Colossians 3:12–14

New clothes for a new lifestyle

It is not enough to get rid of bad habits. We need to be positive and clothe ourselves with new attitudes.

This section begins with 'therefore'. Paul has warned that the Colossians are under attack from false teaching, so they need to be clear about what they believe (that Christ is all and in all), and positive in how they behave (getting rid of old attitudes and negative habits), and *therefore*, when they have stripped off the old clothes, they need to put on the fresh, clean and new ones. Don't stop at blocking off the old habits; replace them at once with new ones. As an encouragement Paul reminds the

Colossians, and us, that the Jews were and are God's chosen people, but so are we – we are chosen in Christ, holy, set apart, dearly loved by God and, we hope, loved by one another. Most of us flourish best when we know we are needed and loved. Many people are immensely lonely, even in Christian fellowships, and find it difficult to feel loved. So it is good to be reminded that we are undergirded with the love of Christ wherever we go.

In the light, then, of God's favour and approval, Paul gives us three positive orders: get dressed, forgive and love.

Get dressed (verse 12)

Paul may have in mind here the rite of baptism, as it seems to have been practised in his time. The new believers took off their old clothes, a sign of stripping off the old life, and were symbolically 'drowned' in the water. They emerged, resurrected to a new life, clean and washed from sin, and put on new clothes, probably white robes. This was to be not the end of the matter but the beginning. These 'new clothes' need to be worn for the rest of one's life. So what attitudes are represented by the new clothes, to replace the old, tattered garments described in verses 8–9?

▶ *Compassion* originally meant 'participation in the suffering of another person', and it still means that today: fellow-feeling, the ability to see and feel things from another person's point of view.

▶ *Kindness* obviously means being gentle and showing consideration for others, a virtue sometimes missing in the most zealous of Christians. It implies having power and yet deliberately refraining from using it.

▶ *Humility*. The false teachers were arrogant and guilty of spiritual pride, anything but humble. Yes, we are God's chosen people, but that fact is a cause for profound thankfulness, never pride. We are not superior to other people.

▶ *Gentleness* does not imply cowardice, sloppiness or the inability to make decisions. It does mean good manners, reliability, and freedom from intensity and from sudden changes of mood.

▶ *Patience.* When we are trying to form a close community embracing people with many different gifts and personalities, how patient we need to be with one another! Paul develops this in verse 13.

This list is an extract from the longer description of the fruit of the Spirit in the letter to the Galatians (5:22–23). These are wonderful virtues, which cannot be manufactured by our own good intentions. They are implanted in us only by God's holy and life-giving Spirit if we will persistently ask for them.

Forgive (verse 13)

Thinking of patience leads Paul to remember how much we need to put up with one another. 'If only we had a new minister!' 'Why can't she see that she's upsetting everyone?' 'However much we tell him, he'll never learn!' 'How can she call herself a Christian and yet do that?' Those exclamation marks and question marks express our exasperation. 'The church would be so much better if everyone was like me,' we may feel. Oh dear! Have we any idea how much forbearance and patience other people are expending on *us*?

When you have a grievance, says Paul, go out of your way to forgive the offender. Forgiveness given grudgingly is not forgiveness at all. A child, when ordered to, may say, with a thunderous look, 'All right, I forgive you', but that is not what she means. Sometimes even Christians will approach this matter with the unspoken attitude, 'You'd better have a good reason for me to forgive you or I won't.' Paul's approach, however, hopes that the offender will have a good reason and, even if not, wants reconciliation. How often do we really give others the benefit of the doubt?

Beware too the hypocrisy of saying,' I forgive you for myself, of course, but God's honour is at stake here and I cannot compromise that.' This is dangerous talk. God's honour is certainly very important, but he can surely take care of it for himself. It's all too easy to posture, pretending to be concerned for God's honour, when really we are just peeved or holding on to a grudge. This is especially a problem when we are dealing with someone we don't naturally like. We can all get on well with our friends. But we are called to get on well with our enemies and with those within our fellowship whom we would never have chosen as friends. Let us at least be honest with ourselves and admit that we don't get on well with So-and-So (and it could be my fault!), rather than pretending that we are defending the Lord's honour in this particular dispute. It was that same Lord who taught us to pray, 'Forgive us our sins, for we also forgive everyone who sins against us' (Luke 11:4).

Love (verse 14)

Now, over all those virtues, which can be seen as a set of undergarments, we are to put on the cloak or overcoat of love. Paul seems to have in mind the idea that the undergarments (in our terms, teeshirts, sweaters, jeans, shirts, jackets, skirts, trousers, etc.) are varied and do not always match very well. A big cloak, fastened with a stout belt, will hold them all together and give our rig-out a proper unity. So in all this talk of behaviour, our distinctively Christian virtue is self-giving love, the love that only God can inspire in us. Make sure, Paul is saying, that you are overwhelmed with this love for one another.

Questions

1. Think about a person with whom you have a difference, perhaps a grudge or any grievance. How far is this a personality clash and how far is it really a matter of

principle? Is it his/her fault, or yours? Does it really matter whose fault it is? How will you solve this problem? (If you can answer this question, remember to act on it without delay!)

2. Look again at the five examples of the Spirit's fruit in verse 12. Discuss how each can be employed in your church or fellowship. Avoid criticizing anyone who is present (and anyone who is not).

3. In what sense were the Jews God's chosen people? Are they still? Some people believe that the Jews have forfeited their privilege because they crucified Jesus. Is this true? In what sense are Christians God's chosen people? Is the rest of humankind not chosen? How do your answers square with John 3:16–17?

Colossians 3:15–17

Live thankfully as the people of God

Jesus Christ is central to the enrichment of our lives together.

After a series of specific do's and don'ts, concluding with the overarching call to love, Paul adds three general principles: 'Let the peace of Christ rule in your hearts', 'Let the word of Christ dwell in you richly' and 'do it all in the name of the Lord Jesus'.

The peace of Christ (verse 15)

In all the ups and downs of everyday life, especially when there are disagreements, we are to let the peace of God be the final arbiter. In games such as tennis, cricket or baseball the umpire or referee makes a series of decisions that allow the game to proceed fairly and smoothly. So our lives together will proceed in harmony if we allow God's peace to be our umpire or referee. The word 'peace' here implies more than a feeling of tranquillity. It means unity, wholesomeness and health. Peace is to be the distinctive feature of the 'body of Christ', God's people.

Christians are so often at loggerheads with one another that it might look as if warfare was the distinctive feature, rather than peace. It has been said that whenever three Christians get together there will be four opinions, the fourth being the correct one. We turn our opinions into principles and make divisions, often totally unnecessarily. The peace of Christ must be allowed to step in and make for unity. To this we are called. And for this we should be heartily, not grudgingly, thankful. The peace and unity of the people of God are more important than that a special opinion should win the argument. This does not imply a papering over of cracks so that we can pretend we are at one; it means allowing the Lord to heal the cracks so that no papering over is necessary.

The word of Christ (verse 16)

The remedy for false teaching is to live at peace together, to affirm one another as we are in Christ and to let the word of Christ dwell in us richly. Wherever the Bible is loved and taught and explained, we find ourselves protected from enemy attack. There are differences of interpretation, of course. There are disputable matters in this letter to the Colossians, things difficult to understand; but when we gather round the word of Christ so clearly expressed in Scripture, it is difficult not to see the truth for ourselves and realize how it applies to our lives, and we find ourselves bound together in unity.

Many of our churches are in danger of producing a biblically deprived generation, and we shall find ourselves more and more a prey to division and strife. We need to become biblically minded, thoroughly soaked in the word, allowing it to 'dwell' in us richly as it flows through all our services and meetings. Occasionally we need to be told off, 'admonished', when our life does not match up to God's standards. This is not a matter of saying, 'You have rocked the fellowship's boat', or 'You have disobeyed the fellowship's leader', but 'You will need to compare your actions and attitudes with God's word.' This must be done with wisdom, careful of the feelings of all involved.

How good it is that so much of what we sing – hymns, choruses, psalms, any kind of spiritual songs – reflects or quotes from Scripture! We sing with gratitude in our hearts. Here again is the thankfulness that Paul expressed in the previous verse. We can express this thankfulness in many and various ways.

The name of Christ (verse 17)

This section ends with a pithy saying of Paul's: 'whatever you do … do it all in the name of the Lord Jesus.' This is one of those golden rules that should always be near the surface of our consciousness. We may not remember all the details discussed in the previous verses, but whatever we do, it should be done in the name of Christ.

It sounds great, but what does it mean? If we cannot claim to be doing something for Jesus, does it mean that we should not be doing it at all? Certainly this text has helped many people who were about to fall for some temptation. Does Jesus really want us to do this? Will he be doing it with us? If we end every prayer with 'in the name of Christ', is it more likely to be answered? But we need to be careful here, because our consciences can be very unpredictable, and it is easy to convince ourselves that the things we really want are in line with God's will. (See 'Manipulating your beliefs', page 64.) Other people may try to make us ashamed of something that Jesus wants us to do. Conversely, in following the Christian crowd we may be following them into what is wrong. So this is a tricky one. Paul was not laying down precise, pharisaical rules, but encouraging us to positive and wholehearted action in the name of Christ and ultimately for his sake.

'Giving thanks.' What, yet again? Paul was never far from gratitude. In all his writings there is an unmistakable air of the breathless excitement of one who can't quite believe that God has chosen him. That rotten Saul of Tarsus, who butchered Christians whenever he could and pursued them in all directions, the 'chief of sinners', as he described himself – that *he* could receive God's grace staggered him till his dying day, and he was immensely and constantly grateful. So whatever we do or wherever we go – walking together, drinking coffee, enjoying meals, attending meetings, working, playing, praying or weeping – we can do it all in the name of Jesus and with thanksgiving.

Questions

1. What is involved in letting the word of God dwell in us richly? Reading the Bible sensibly and regularly is a start. But how, and with what attitude and what expectations?
2. Make a short list of behaviours that some Christians approve of and others do not. How can we decide whether we can do these things 'in the name of the Lord Jesus' and with thanksgiving? How reliable is conscience as a guide?
3. Paul calls us to be thankful at all times. In his letter to the Ephesians (5:20), however, he goes further, and says that we should be thankful 'for everything'. Is it right to give thanks for unpleasant, even evil, things? What sort of things should we be thankful for? Does our temperament come into this, so that some people have a more grateful nature than others? How can we help one another to live more gratefully (without being 'holier than thou')?

Colossians 3:18 – 4:1

Personal relationships

Sound teaching and committed faith need to be demonstrated in loving and thoughtful relationships.

It is relatively easy to make wise statements about peace and thankfulness and obeying God's word, but the test comes when we have to translate the theory into everyday living and that means getting on well with people. Paul now turns to three pairs of close relationships: wives and husbands, children and parents, and slaves and masters. In each case he takes first the category perceived to be the weaker: wives, children, slaves. He makes a statement about them which would have been readily accepted at the time, and follows this up with a revolutionary idea. This is a fascinating piece of pastoral writing, showing Paul's care and sensitivity towards all six groups of people.

Wives and husbands (verses 18–19)

'Wives, submit to your husbands' simply repeated commonly held wisdom in the ancient world, with a Christian slant added: 'as is fitting in the Lord'. It soon becomes clear, however, that Paul is not parroting the usual rigid male chauvinism of the time: the tyranny of the husband, the subjugation of the wife, and the abuse of women in general. He goes straight into a revolutionary command: 'Husbands, love your wives and do not be harsh with them.'

This would produce gasps of amazement. Most first-century husbands would be scandalized. 'You leave me alone, Paul. I'll deal with my wife as I want to, thank you very much. She's *my* wife, not yours. You don't even have a wife, do you?' Paul was saying something new. He may well have been sowing the seeds of the emancipation of women which has been so long in coming.

Many husbands still need this simple but gentle reminder. Christian husbands are no less guilty of wife-abuse today than non-believing husbands or partners. In fact, some use the first phrase of Paul's order as an excuse to ignore the second. Husbands can so easily take their wives for granted. The passion and commitment they once felt may have dwindled into a relationship of convenience where two people live together under the same roof. Paul expects kindness and a deep, committed love. He is not talking primarily about emotion here, but about a determination to treat wives with the utmost care, consideration and courtesy.

Children and parents (verses 20–21)

'Children, obey your parents in everything.' Of course. Children had no rights at all in the ancient world. We might say that legally they were not yet people. As long as the father was still alive, the son was in submission to him by Roman law. This obedience, says Paul, is pleasing to the Lord. Why? Because if children do not learn to obey their parents, how will they learn to obey God?

But then comes Paul's hand-grenade, which explodes among the fathers reading or listening to this letter: 'Do not embitter your children.' Don't wind them up or discourage them. What an odd thought! The wealthy often ignored their children and had them brought up by nannies and tutors. The poor were too busy scratching out a living to have time for the subtleties of child-rearing. Children often grew up brutalized. Here was a totally new approach, a new beginning. Yet when we consider Dickensian London with its chimney-climbing boys and pickpockets, poor houses and brutal schools, and the treatment of street children and child prostitutes in many parts of the world today, we wonder how long it will be before Paul's words sink in.

Slaves and masters (3:22 – 4:1)

'Slaves, obey your earthly masters in everything.' What else could they do? This is not a question of what slaves should do, but how they do it. Do it willingly, not because you are forced to obey, but with a changed attitude now you are in Christ. Both you and your masters will have to answer to a greater Master one day in heaven (verse 1). Again it may be that Paul is sowing the seeds of emancipation at this point. That process took eighteen hundred years to come to fruition, and is still by no means universal (see the studies in Philemon, pages 106ff.).

Verses 22–25 apply very appropriately to all workers today on land, on sea or in the air, in the home, the office or the street, or, if it comes to that, in the church. In the workplace we are called upon to give a fair day's work for a fair day's wages. It is right for us to be in submission to the authorities, although the company or the boss does not own our soul. Over and above the biggest multinational stands the power of the living God, whose standards and values we are called upon to live by.

Many people are watching us, as we live out our relationships in the family and the workplace, to see whether our Christian profession really works. So, runs Paul's argument, this kind of lifestyle will defeat false teaching because it demonstrates all that we have learned about what Jesus Christ came to live and die for. We must therefore make sure that no-one can blame us in respect of our family, marriage or work environment, and that our life is beyond reproach.

Questions

1. Men and women are clearly of equal value before God, but can a husband–wife relationship ever be one of

equality in every respect? How should we interpret 'Wives, submit to your husbands' today? Read 'Paul and women' below before you answer this one.

2. Share in the group your experiences of being a child and relating to your own and other people's children. This part of the discussion may need to be cut short or there will be no time for the question: how can children be taught to obey in today's culture, which offers them rights but not duties?

3. How can we live honestly in the workplace if our colleagues are intent on stealing time and equipment or damaging people's reputations? How far should we turn a blind eye, or risk exclusion if we report malpractice? Give examples.

Paul and women

The popular image of Paul as a woman-hater is simply not true to the facts. As we have just seen, he was in many ways the great liberator of women in the ancient world. Certainly he reflected the views of his time – 'Wives, obey your husbands' – but he balanced that with the revolutionary command, 'Husbands, love your wives.'

This twenty-first-century world sneers at such outmoded advice as 'Wives, obey your husbands', and prefers unmarried partnership to traditional marriage. Christians are faced with a difficult question here. Did Paul give this order merely because he was living in the first century and did not know any better? Or is this a basic, universal rule of God for all time, which has been abandoned by modern men and women? It should be acknowledged that other religions have often kept to this marriage principle more faithfully than Christianity.

Our answer to the question will depend largely on how we view the divine inspiration of Paul's words. Do we take every word literally at face value because it is

Scripture, or are we at liberty to interpret the scriptural principles behind what he says and apply them to our own situation? For example, when we read, 'it is disgraceful for a woman to speak in the church' (1 Corinthians 14:35), we are inclined to argue that Paul was respecting the Jewish custom of his day (he has appealed to Jewish law in the previous verse), and assume that, if he were with us today, he would have explained more clearly what he meant, or not even mentioned it at all. Similarly, the whole discussion of women covering their heads when they pray or prophesy (1 Corinthians 11:3–16) appears to be irrelevant to us today. A few women still wear hats in church in obedience to the letter of this law, but most ignore it completely. Would it not be better to take the principle behind the example seriously – the principle that we should always show a proper respect for the customs which prevail today?

Following this line of interpretation, many Christians would say, 'Yes, take this injunction of Paul's seriously, but not absolutely literally. View the word 'obey' in the light of modern customs and expectations. Follow the spirit, rather than the letter, of the law. We need to be very careful, however, before we decide that a command from Paul is 'culturally determined' and therefore not to be interpreted literally. Certainly he reflected the customs of his day; how could he have done otherwise? But it is very hard for us to know where customs of the day end and God's universal commands begin. Some biblical injunctions must be translated into the lifestyle of our own day, but the problem is to know where to draw the line. It would be possible to explain away the whole Bible as 'culturally determined', with no relevance to us today at all. These are questions that demand study, prayer and humility on all sides.

Christian households

In modern society, 'family' can mean many different things. We have to apply the principles that Paul is laying down to, for instance,

▶ believers married to unbelieving partners

▶ families that include second or subsequent marriages

▶ cohabiting partnerships or long-term boyfriend /girlfriend relationships

▶ one-parent families

▶ stepchildren and step-parents

Paul gives the impression that each of these commands is to be unconditional; that is, obeyed regardless of the other's response. We may wish that he had written, 'Husbands, love wives as long as they love you in return.' But in any human relationship there may come a time when we can continue no further. How far should a wife or child submit to harsh or abusive treatment? What does it mean to 'embitter your children'? And if a Christian parent does embitter his or her children, what can be done about it?

We are familiar with the idea that Scripture should be read aloud in services of worship, but we may well have a comfortable feeling that what Paul was writing to the Colossians is not directed at us. But this letter was read aloud to the church to which it was addressed. Can we imagine the impact of an epistle about family relationships in our own church being read aloud on Sunday morning?

Questions raised in this section need to be brought into your discussion of this passage.

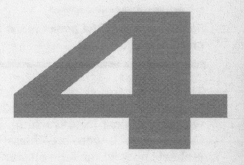

MAKE CHRIST
WIDELY KNOWN

Colossians 4:2–18

Colossians 4:2–4

The priority of prayer

Faithful and watchful prayer is the foundation for all clear presentation of Christ.

The central thrust of Paul's letter has been the exaltation of Jesus and earnest warning against false teaching. He now moves on, as it were breathlessly: 'Time is short ; now let me tell you some things vitally important for your spiritual health.' It is as if he has changed gear from theological precision to pastoral passion. The sentences are shorter. The mood is urgent. His time may be desperately short. Now this is true for us as well. We easily fall into the trap of feeling that tomorrow is soon enough to respond to the claims of Jesus Christ. Tomorrow, of course, never comes. God above knows how much time we have left. So we need to devote ourselves to prayer.

Devote yourselves to prayer (verse 2)

The word 'devote' is used ten times in the New Testament. The form of the word carries the flavour of continuing action: 'Go on going on with what you have committed yourself to.' A related word, used in the Old Testament, means, 'give up utterly to God's use or purpose'. A sacrifice was described as 'devoted to God'. Putting these two ideas together suggests that prayer ought to be our permanent obsession. The seventeenth-century monk Brother Lawrence used to 'practise the presence of God' wherever he was. Certainly we need special times of prayer, but we can also learn to *live* prayerfully.

While Christians down the ages have found their spiritual lives have flourished under the discipline of setting aside a regular time for Bible study and prayer, many people today dislike adhering to rules and following a fixed daily pattern. They have abandoned the old habit (some would call it 'tyranny') of the daily 'quiet time' of prayer. Old sayings like 'No Bible, no breakfast', and 'Don't let your head touch the pillow if you haven't had your nose in the Book', seem laughable in their rigidity. Abandoning empty ritual is good as long as it is replaced by something better. The danger is that it will be replaced with nothing at all. Prayerlessness and carelessness in the end make us very ineffective Christians. If we are to abandon the quiet time, we must replace it with a passion for prayer in place of the duty to pray.

This involves being watchful, staying awake and being alert. Paul may have had in mind what he had heard about the disciples' Gethsemane experience, when they had slept when Jesus had called them to watch; or the transfiguration, when again they were asleep and almost missed the glorious vision (see Mark 14:32–42 and Luke 9:28–36). 'Be on your guard.' This is a command to us all, not just as individuals but also as a church, to make prayer your goal. Active and energetic churches are in danger of missing out on the quiet 'waiting on God' that is so necessary (see 'Prayer: a combined operation', page 93). And be thankful. Again? Yes, even if it sounds boring. Be thankful!

Pray for us (verse 3)

Prayer letters are a familiar ingredient of many postbags, especially at Christmas time. We are offered plenty of information on which to base our prayers for missionaries, ministers, friends and relations. Their needs cry out to us. What should we expect Paul to major on in this prayer letter? 'Pray that I'll get out of these wretched chains; that my guards will be nice to me; that the food will improve'? No, none of those things. Many of our prayer meetings focus on making us all happier, warmer and fitter. But

Paul's chief concern was that the door should be open to the message of the gospel. His guards came in and out of an open door. He could not follow them because of his chains. But the 'mystery' of Christ, the message 'Christ in you, the hope of glory', is not chained and knows no boundaries.

Prayer, like the gospel, is an intercontinental missile. It could cross the distance from Paul to Colosse and back in a split second. It can range throughout the world. This is a great encouragement to us in our limited circumstances. Many of us feel frustrated because we cannot do much for the gospel. We may not be bound by chains as Paul was, but we may be hemmed in by health problems, social circumstances, the needs of our children, the dependence of elderly relatives, housing problems, lack of knowledge ('I'm no theologian') … But the fact is that the gospel is not limited by our circumstances. And it is released by the power of prayer. And this is how we can be involved whoever, whenever and wherever we are. There is passion in Paul's cry. The gospel matters and our prayers can release it, so that the message may have an open door. What a challenge! What a responsibility! What a privilege!

Pray for a clear presentation of the truth (verse 4)

No matter how earnestly we pray or how carefully we prepare our gospel message it will do no good at all if people cannot hear it and hear it clearly. They must be able not only to hear the truth but also to understand it. There's no use confusing people with complicated sermons or vague ideas, however interesting they may be to us, if the hearers are not left with something solid to hold on to.

Paul is always anxious to assure us that the message is Christ and not Paul. A major obstacle to the clarity of the gospel may be the messenger, getting in the way of the message. There is a danger that what is communicated may be identified with the person who preaches it: Luís Palau's gospel, Billy Graham's gospel, Paul's gospel. No, the focus must be on Christ alone. May we be delivered from the arrogance of thinking that we are doing rather well as preachers or housegroup leaders, and that it would be best for people to come to faith through us rather than by some other route! This is especially a danger if we have been to some big convention or an inspiring training course, and we return ready to put everyone else right. But the solution to our church's problems lies not in us but in Jesus Christ, humbly and clearly presented. This is what we need to be praying for, persistently and devotedly.

Questions

1. Take stock of your own prayer habits. Do you pray when you feel like it? When you don't feel like it? How far are you 'devoted to prayer'? How do Paul's words in this section come across to you?
2. What exactly is prayer? In what sense can it be said to 'work'? What do we expect prayer to achieve?
3. Given a limited amount of time, is it better to read over before the Lord a list of the names of the people we want to pray for, or to concentrate on one person, trying to imagine his/her problems and joys and asking God to meet those specific needs? Share your experiences.

Prayer: a combined operation

As a church, Paul tells us, we need to make prayer our goal. But how? Today it is recognized that personality plays a large part in the kind of prayer that we can manage. Some people are 'doers' by nature and others 'reflectors'. It is much more complicated in fact, but this is basically true. 'Doers' will find difficulty with meditation and contemplation. If they set aside a day to meditate on the word of God, they may read a chapter from the Bible and, ninety seconds later, say, 'I've done that. What do I do now?' Such people pray more naturally with others, through worshipping together and through activity. Others may feel that they have really prayed only when they have shut everyone else out and spent time getting quiet and focused. Only then are they able to be lost in wonder, love and praise. Others again may be neither activist 'doers' nor mystical 'reflectors', but hard-headed folk who can see that a job needs doing, like praying for twenty friends and relations. They set aside a disciplined time for doing it, keep to that time and faithfully work through the list. They haven't done anything, or even felt anything, but the job was accomplished.

There are many varieties of personality types, but all of us can pray. We need one another to support us in our different approaches, not to condemn us for not praying 'properly' (that is, the way I do it!). A prayer group or worship committee needs to face these very real differences in the way we approach our praying, arrange a programme to suit differing needs and give opportunities to people to explore less familiar ways of praying. They can share ideas and helps, such as praying aloud to keep the mind from wandering, or praying while walking or while sitting in a particular chair (for those who find routines helpful); praying through passages of the Bible (for those who prefer a formal structure); or writing down one's prayers in a prayer journal. By these means we may help one another to be more devoted to prayer.

Colossians 4:5–6

Living the good news

Paul gives valuable tips about relating to non-believers.

 The urgent mood of the last section of this letter, prior to the final greetings, continues with four pithy principles for living out the gospel.

Be wise in the way you act (verse 5)

The 'outsiders' are looking at us, so we need to act particularly wisely. We are living samples of Christ's family, and the world in general already has the idea that we're a pretty odd lot. Things have not changed. The ancient world called Christians 'atheists' because they didn't have gods as other people did (the concept of one true God was beyond their understanding). They were accused of cannibalism. (They met behind closed doors and ate bodies and drank blood, didn't they?) Outsiders often look at us with amazement because they have no idea why we behave as we do.

The temptation that challenges us at this point is to hide what we believe or to compromise our Christian lifestyle to fit in with what is generally acceptable to the outside world. Paul was certainly willing to be all things to everyone so that some might be saved (see 1 Corinthians 9:22), but he did not mean that we should go along with the crowd to save our embarrassment. Some clergy have won applause by getting drunk with the lads on Saturday night, but it is doubtful whether the gospel has spread very widely by these means! We cannot deal with sin by promoting it. We have to walk the tightrope, neither cutting ourselves off from non-believers, nor falling into their ways of life. This requires wisdom. We must be spiritual, but spirituality does not mean stupidity.

Make the most of every opportunity (verse 5)

The time is short. Snap up the bargains. At sale time, stores offer huge reductions in the prices of their goods. The crowds gather round the door long before opening time. Then there is a great surge as the doors open and people rush for the best bargains. They fight each other for goods which they may not actually want, but will buy simply because they are bargains. The bargain Paul has in mind, however, is of great value to all Christians: the chance to speak to someone about our faith.

Some of us are very discouraged about this business of personal evangelism. We get so embarrassed and guilt-ridden about it that we fail to recognize the opportunities when they arise. There is only one group more frightened of evangelism than non-Christians, and that is Christians! This is because we feel, or we have been taught, that we ought to force the conversation round to 'Christian things'. This, of course, is unnatural. We are embarrassed and so are our friends, and a barrier is erected. In most cases, therefore, unless we have a God-given gift (and some have), we should never force opportunities to speak of Jesus, but we should be on the watch for them and snap them up graciously and lovingly when they appear.

Live salty lives (verse 6)

'Conversation' here means much more than talking to someone. It includes our very way of life. Well-chosen words may accomplish much, but a richly seasoned relationship counts for much more. A story is told of a young man who joined the Navy. He fell desperately in love with a young woman and they were engaged on the day he set sail for a year's cruise. He wrote her a postcard every day, expressing his love for her. At the end of the year, when he came back, there was a happy marriage. The young woman married the postman!

To be practical, it may be helpful to carry with us a simple tract or booklet which explains the way to salvation better than we could. A pocket Bible is also a valuable friend. When we speak to people, and as we live alongside them, we need to convey grace and warmth, never bitterness or abrasiveness, so that the 'salt' in our lifestyle may bring out the flavour in theirs.

Know how to answer everyone (verse 6)

Peter famously wrote, 'Always be prepared to give an answer to everyone who asks you to give the reason for the hope that you have. But do this with gentleness and respect' (1 Peter 3:15–16). Paul makes the same plea here. To know what we believe and why is of great importance, both for our own assurance and also for the benefit of those who ask us about our faith. It may seem a daunting task to prepare ourselves to answer any question that outsiders may throw at us – if not impossible. However, almost all the basic questions that arise are about hypocrisy, science, suffering, the Bible, Jesus and a few more. If we can grasp these basics we may well be equipped to mount a defence of why or what we believe.

Equally, many in the 'I'm no theologian' bracket are unable or unwilling to study at this depth, and yet may be better advertisements for the faith than those who can master complicated and compelling arguments. It has been said that a person with an experience is rarely at the mercy of a person with an argument. Peter called upon his readers to defend the hope that they had, not to explain the doctrines of the apostolic fathers. It is often more helpful, even impressive, to be able to say, 'My hope is based on Jesus because he loves me and he's never let me down', than to expound the Nicene Creed. In other words, we should try hard to explain clearly as much of our faith as we can, but often a simple, personal, experience-based testimony is more effective. We should always be willing to admit when we are out of our depth. 'I don't know the answer to that, but I will try to find it, if you like.' A humble attitude is worth a hundred words, and a very humble attitude is worth a thousand.

Questions

1. You are travelling in a railway carriage. Do you speak to other passengers about your faith? Do you speak about anything at all? Should you feel guilty if you don't? Does it depend on how much you know about God? Or whether you are a shy person or naturally outgoing? Or whether others seem to want to talk? Share experiences with the group, referring back to verses 5–6.
2. Make a list of the questions outsiders are likely to ask us as Christians. Which of them could we answer with confidence? How ought we to cope with the others?
3. Press (!) two volunteers to role-play before the group a Christian talking to an enquiring outsider. Ask for the group's comments. Get others to have a turn in the hot seats. Summarize together what you have learned.

Colossians 4:7–15

Partners in the gospel

A network of Christian friends is drawn closer by the sending of greetings and the exchange of news.

The letters we possess in the New Testament are obviously just the tip of an iceberg. The invisible part of the communication, now lost to us, was by word of

mouth. Tychicus was to tell the Colossians all the news about Paul; so there was to be a verbal report as well as the written one. Perhaps Tychicus would read the letter aloud to the assembled church and give a running commentary as he did so. Paul seems to have employed a network of faithful messengers who spoke on his behalf. He was very close to them and they seem to have understood him well. They knew the churches to which Paul wrote and were always glad to send their own greetings.

So here is Paul's list of friends and fellow-workers who send their greetings. It is remarkably similar to the list in the letter to Philemon. (See pages 116–117 for more information, not all of which is repeated here.)

Tychicus (verses 7–8). Paul affirms him. He is a dear brother, a faithful minister and fellow-servant in the Lord. He is not just the messenger boy. So they should listen to him and all that he has to say to encourage their hearts. In the first place it would be a joy to them to know that Paul was still alive. Months may have gone by without news; there was no such thing as e-mail, newspapers, telephones, radio or TV. Tychicus would tell them not only that was Paul alive and kicking but also that his imprisonment was not too irksome. It was probably more like a house-arrest, and Paul did have freedom to talk to his friends, despite his chains. There was much to be thankful for.

Onesimus (verse 9). The letter to Philemon is all about Onesimus the slave. Briefly, he had run away from Philemon, his master in Colosse, had found Paul and had become a Christian. Now he was being sent back. There is a hint here that the two letters that we know as Colossians and Philemon were being sent together to Colosse. It is significant that Onesimus is described here as a faithful and dear brother, not as a runaway slave. The slave aspect was now irrelevant, even the fact that he had run away. His credentials were not tarnished. Onesimus must have been thrilled to hear his name mentioned alongside that of Tychicus. He had been raised from the status of slave to that of a partner in the gospel. This is a point worth pondering when we feel depressed about our own lack of status or when we feel worthless.

Aristarchus (verse 10). The word 'fellow-prisoner' is probably symbolic (Aristarchus and Paul were both imprisoned by the ties of the gospel), but they might both have been literally in prison. Aristarchus was always in the thick of the action (see, for example, the part he played in the Ephesus riot, Acts 19:23–41). He was not one of those who knocked off when the going was tough. He was committed to Paul and stood with him literally. May God grant us all Christian friends who will stay with us in good times and bad, and help us to be equally faithful to others!

Mark (verse 10). Mark had let Paul down badly (see Acts 15:36–41, and page 116). Barnabas had stepped in and reconciled the antagonists; and now Paul, not holding a grudge against Mark, commends him to the church at Colosse. It is a significant sign of maturity in Christian leadership when you can commend those who have let you down and failed you. Of course, it would be naïve and irresponsible to give such people jobs they are not capable of doing, but to be given a second chance, a way back to full fellowship and responsibility, is a very healing and encouraging experience. Mark was back!

Jesus, who is called Justus (verse 11). We know nothing further about him. Both 'Jesus' and 'Justus' were common names in the first century. He was a Jew, one of the few who still supported Paul.

Epaphras (verses 12–13), the man who planted the church in Colosse. There is a hint here that he may have fallen out with his own people, and Paul is anxious to recommend him. The senior apostle backs up his junior friend without reservation. In fact, Epaphras had been hard at work for all the local churches in the Lycus valley.

Luke (verse 14). Our dear old friend Doctor Luke! It is possible that Luke had given up a thriving practice to join Paul's team. There is evidence that Paul suffered from a chronic medical complaint. He calls it his 'thorn in the flesh' in 2 Corinthians 12:7. It would have been a great comfort to him to have a doctor among his band of followers.

Demas (verse 14). See pages 116–117.

After the greetings from his friends, Paul sends his Christian love specifically to the church at Laodicea and emphasizes that the letter must be sent on to them. They must have faced the same set of problems as the Colossians. He mentions Nympha and her house church. Where was that, in Colosse or Laodicea? We do not know. She may have been a wealthy woman whose patronage allowed the church to meet in her home. She may have been the leader of the church. Who knows?

It is heart-warming to read of these faithful and loving friends who trusted one another and forgave and supported one another. Many of us have cause to rejoice because some man or woman gave us the same sort of trust that Paul gave Epaphras, Aristarchus, Onesimus, Timothy, Mark – the list could go on and on. Thank God that we're not going to heaven on our own!

Questions

1. Make a list of the people who have been particularly encouraging to you through your life, and give thanks for each one of them.
2. As a group, compile a short letter, as if to a friend, sending news and giving encouragement in Christ. How can you avoid sounding over-pious? (This is particularly a problem when we send a general letter to people with different approaches to faith.) What sort of news do people really want to receive? Do not begin, 'How time flies! It seems like only yesterday when I wrote to you last.'
3. Look again at each of the people mentioned in these verses. Make a list of the characteristics of each one, noting how different they are. Reflect on the differing gifts that you find in your own fellowship or church, and on how you complement one another.

Colossians 4:16–18

Final instructions and greeting

Don't give up. Keep going, and may God's smile rest upon you.

It would be very interesting to read the letter that Paul wrote to Laodicea. Unfortunately, it has been lost. If this letter to Colosse was to be urgently forwarded to Laodicea ('see that it is also read in the church of the Laodiceans'), it is clear that their problems were similar, as we have already noted (and see 2:1).

Now we do have a letter to the church in Laodicea, dating probably from the end of the first century, sent by John and recorded in Revelation 3:14–22. The Lord's message to them was that they had become lukewarm in their faith. They revelled in their material wealth but did not realize their real poverty. This could well describe a church that had been infected by the kind of false teaching that Paul had in mind, perhaps forty years earlier. The teaching had done what he feared it would; blinded the minds of the believers to their true state and made them complacent. Did this happen too at Colosse? We do not know. But even at Laodicea all was not lost. Revelation 3:20 contains some of the most memorable statements in the whole Bible, holding out a lifeline to those compromised and compromising people: 'Here I am! I stand at the door and knock. If anyone hears my voice and opens the door, I will go in and eat with him, and he with me.'

Finish the job (verse 17)

Archippus may have been the son of Philemon (see page

108). It looks as if he had some kind of special work to do in the area, and had somehow begun to pull back. Paul is saying, in effect, 'Archippus, you're a fellow-worker; you've been entrusted with the task. Don't give up now.'

The gifts of perseverence, faithfulness and loyalty are sometimes missing in today's churches, but are, if anything, more necessary than the more spectacular gifts. As the great nineteenth-century preacher Charles Spurgeon said, 'By perseverence the snail reached the ark.' It may be that we find ourselves in mind-blowingly difficult situations, discouraged, disappointed and on the verge of giving up. We need God's grace of recommissioning for the clear task to which we have been called. Tired bodies need new strength and hungry spirits need to be refilled. So we need quietly to go on going on. The end of the tunnel may be nearer than we think. The churches may be full of people who have begun tasks and not finished them. But we need not be among them.

Farewell (verse 18)

Paul has been dictating his letter, probably to Tychicus, or whoever had the neatest handwriting. Now he signs off in his own hand, perhaps with a flourish. As he does so the chain rattles on his wrist and he adds almost the first self-indulgent sentence in the whole letter: 'Remember my chains.' This letter had a freedom that its author did not possess. It could go to his friends when he could not.

And finally, 'Grace be with you.' May God's smile rest upon you. The day is coming when we shall no longer need to say, 'Grace be with you', because grace will be permanently with us and the greeting will be redundant. But, until that time, may the Lord be with us all!

Questions

1. The churches of Laodicea and Colosse seem to have worked together. What are the advantages of working

with a neighbouring church? Do they outweigh the dis-
advantages, such as all the extra work involved? Look
at John 17:22–23.

2. It is said that some people are initiators and others are
finishers. Each kind needs the other. Discuss some practical matters in your church that need constant attention
(such as the stewardship of money, the fabric of the
building, cleaning, tea-and-coffee-making). How can
initiators and finishers best work together without constant friction?

3. Read aloud to the group the section 'Colossians in a
nutshell' on page 20. Then get each member to write
down one aspect of the study which has impressed
him/her most. Read your findings to one another and
discuss them if appropriate.

PHILEMON

Who was Philemon?

As we were reminded at the beginning of the Colossians guide (page 22), reading other people's correspondence, especially from many years ago, leaves us with only one end of the conversation. If we piece together the jigsaw of hints and clues in this short letter to Philemon, the picture that emerges is something like this.

Philemon was a church leader in the little town of Colosse. He was the head of a family, perhaps reasonably well off, and owned slaves, as was usual for someone in his situation. One of these slaves, Onesimus, had, for some reason, run away. He may also have stolen money from his master. Onesimus had made his way to Paul, who was in prison. Perhaps he had realized the enormity of what, in haste, he had done, and wanted advice. Paul was able to give him not only advice but the chance of a new life, and Onesimus became a Christian. He made himself very useful to Paul. However, it would have been illegal, as well as unfair, to keep another man's slave; so Paul wanted Onesimus to return to his rightful owner.

Paul writes this covering letter to ask Philemon, out of the goodness of his heart, to receive Onesimus back. He is now not only a repentant slave, but also a Christian, and therefore in that sense a brother. Under the circumstances, Paul's request is a very tall order, and we shall see how carefully and tactfully Paul sets about his task.

Philemon 1–7

Greetings and thanksgiving

Paul opens his letter with prayer and encouragement, and warm appreciation of his fellow-worker.

This is the shortest of Paul's letters in the New Testament, though longer than most others of his time. It fits exactly in time, place and address with Paul's letter to the Colossians, and we might prefer to find it on the next page in the Bible. The compilers of the New Testament, however, saw fit to tuck it in between Titus and Hebrews, so that is where we find it today.

Greetings (verses 1–3)

As usual, in letters of that time, the writer introduces himself at the beginning and sends greetings, good wishes and, in a Christian letter, prayers. As in his letter to the Colossians, Paul includes Timothy as co-author. He names members of Philemon's household and indeed the whole church as recipients of the letter, but it soon becomes plain that this is a personal appeal from one man to another, Paul to Philemon.

'A prisoner of Jesus Christ' (verse 1). This is the only place where Paul describes himself in this way. He is writing from prison (see Colossians 4:18), even though he hopes soon to be released (Philemon 22), but he leaves out his usual title of 'apostle'. Why? Probably because this is not a letter of command with the authority of Christ through his ambassador, but a moving appeal from one human being in need, on behalf of another (see verses 8–10).

Philemon was obviously a respected citizen of Colosse, owner of slaves and of a house large enough to accommodate a 'house church'. Purpose-built church premises were as yet unheard of (see page 110). It has even been suggested that the whole Colossian church met in Philemon's house and that he was the leader of it. Paul writes to him on equal terms as 'dear friend and fellow-worker'. Apphia was probably Philemon's wife (Paul's use of the word 'sister' is of course shorthand for 'sister in Christ'). Archippus may well have been their son. Again Paul places himself alongside a 'fellow-soldier' (verse 2).

The undeserved love of God ('grace') and the resulting wholeness of spirit that we experience when we receive it ('peace') are the usual greetings in Paul's letters, but this is no merely formal set of words. We may be sure that he means what he writes. Notice that he brackets 'God our Father' with 'the Lord Jesus Christ'. Paul was in no doubt that Jesus Christ was God. It is hard for us to understand how Jesus can be both God and human at the same time; we are inclined to concentrate either on his humanity ('he was one of us') or his divinity ('one with the Father'). The New Testament is clear, however, that he was both.

Thanks and prayers (verses 4–7)

Paul seems to be in no hurry to come to the point – or if he is, he is careful not to leave out necessary preparation. So he encourages Philemon by telling him how he has appeared in Paul's prayers. It is heart-warming for us to learn that people remember us in prayer, especially if they are able to thank God regularly for us. If we do pray for others and give thanks for them, perhaps we should tell them so. It will warm their hearts just as Paul's letter must have affected Philemon.

What Paul actually meant by his prayer (verse 6) is very difficult to understand. Look at a few different Bible versions and see how they tackle it. The New International Version has, 'I pray that you may be active in sharing your faith, so that you will have a full understanding of every good thing we have in Christ.' That seems to mean, 'Tell other people about Jesus Christ. If you do you will have the key to understanding what good things he has in store for us.' But Paul does not mean that. 'Share' means to divide up between oneself and others. So sharing our faith does not mean telling other people about it, as it has come to be understood in Christian circles today. It means getting together to experience our faith, working it out in fellowship with one another. In other words, 'Work together in Christ. Don't try to go it alone. Then you will come to realize what it's all about.'

It looks as if Philemon was already well on the way to being an answer to Paul's prayer. This man from Colosse had a reputation as an encourager and refresher of the hearts of the saints. His fellow-believers were no doubt hard-pressed and bewildered by the teachings of some, which conflicted with Paul's own teaching. Philemon stands out as a man to whom they could come and pour out their problems and go away refreshed. What a wonderful reputation to have!

Questions

1. An individual exercise. Write down the names of half-a-dozen friends or family members. Beside each name list the things you have done or said recently which will have encouraged them, built them up or made them feel valued. Then write another list of more things you might say or do to build them up yet further. Pray through your lists and decide how to act.
2. What are the dangers and what are the benefits of people using their gifts individually? In what ways can we share, that is, work out, our faith together?
3. How important is it that we have a church building? What does it mean to you? What should it be like? How will it affect those we want to draw in? If you have time, design an ideal church building, best for God, for the fellowship and for outsiders.

'The church that meets in your home'

First-century Jews worshipped in purpose-built synagogues, and Christian Jews often continued to attend. But Christians needed to celebrate the Lord's Supper and to pray together and encourage one another in their new faith. Church buildings were as yet unknown, so it was natural to meet in a home that was large enough to contain 'the gathering together of the Lord's people', in other words, the church. The earliest church building so far discovered dates from AD 232–33 and is in Dura-Europos in Syria. Even that was originally a house, later adapted for use as a chapel.

The 'house-church' arrangement was more than a convenient roof to worship under, however. A vivid description of the New Testament church was the 'household of faith'. Every ordinary family had its head, and God the Father (or sometimes Jesus Christ) was seen as the head of the Christian household, his church. Sometimes the church is spoken of as the 'body of Christ', and he is described as its head. Christians saw themselves as related to one another. When Paul calls Apphia his 'sister' he means to imply that they have both been adopted into the family of God, and are therefore related by close spiritual ties. The mutual support that a family was expected to provide would be even more important to the young church, struggling for existence or flexing its new muscles in a hostile world.

The close relationship between the family of Philemon and the family/household nature of the church that met in his home shines clearly through this little letter. Philemon seems to have acted as a father to the Christians, a pointer to their true Father in heaven.

If you want to study this family idea further, here are a few of the many New Testament references: Galatians

6:10; Ephesians 3:14–15; Hebrews 13:1; 1 Peter 1:23; 1 John 3:9 ('born of God' into his new family); 1 Corinthians 3:1–2; Ephesians 1:5; Romans 8:17.

Philemon 8–21

Paul's urgent plea for Onesimus

Paul's request that Philemon should receive Onesimus back 'as a brother' is a masterpiece of tact and sensitivity.

Gradually, carefully, Paul edges nearer to the point of his letter. We almost feel like saying, 'Oh, come on Paul, out with it!' Philemon's eye had probably scanned the page by now, and he knew what was coming. In fact, Onesimus himself had probably just handed him the letter. As it was an open letter to the whole church, Philemon would have to respond in public. Paul tactfully prepares the ground.

Paul bends over backwards (verses 8–9)

Why does Paul appeal to Philemon 'on the basis of love' and not by the command of an apostle? Perhaps he knew that Philemon reacted badly to being ordered about. Perhaps Paul felt that, as an apostle, he had Christ's authority only in matters central to the inheritance of the faith; detailed questions like this were for personal decision. Anyway, he continues to appeal to Philemon's better nature: 'I'm an old man and I'm in prison; you won't let me down, will you?' He almost overdoes it. Come off it, Paul, you surely can't be as old as all that!

Paul comes to the point (verses 10–14)

At last it all tumbles out. 'I appeal to you for my son Onesimus.' Oh, so *that's* what it's all about! But wait a minute: Onesimus, your *son*! It would have been amazing to learn that the slave had found Paul at all (even if Paul was at Ephesus, the distance was a hundred miles or so). It was even more astonishing, and heart-warming, to hear that the runaway had become a Christian believer. 'Onesimus' means 'useful', a common name for a slave – perhaps originally a nickname. Paul loved to play with words, and verse 11 is quite a complicated little puzzle (see below, page 118).

Onesimus had attached himself to Paul, and had become not only a great help to him in his imprisonment but also a good friend, indeed a son. Paul refers to Timothy as his son (1 Timothy 1:2), born anew through the older man's testimony. Son or not, Paul was right in not holding on to Onesimus, because he still belonged as a slave to Philemon. So the decision is with the slave-owner – a free decision, not a compulsion: 'Will you have Onesimus back, or shall he return to me?', Paul is saying in effect.

Paul prompts Philemon's decision (verses 15–16)

Almost before Philemon has had time to think about his answer, Paul is suggesting that Onesimus's real place is back in Colosse. 'He is very dear to me but even dearer to you, both as a man and as a brother in the Lord' (verse 16). A slave, a thief, a deserter and now a man and indeed a brother! No wonder Paul has been writing carefully and tactfully, preparing the ground. It was like being asked to receive a burglar who has ransacked your house as a long-lost son-in-law. We wish we could have seen Philemon's face as he read this letter, especially if Onesimus was standing meekly by.

It is very unlikely that Paul was hinting that Onesimus should be freed from slavery at this point. Warm relationships often existed between owners and slaves, and in

Christ they would be brothers even across the 'ownership barrier'(look at Ephesians 6:5–9, for example).

Paul offers to foot the bill (verses 17–21)

'If he has done you any wrong' (surely he had, by running away in the first place) 'or owes you anything …' (verse 18). Some think Paul was unsure of what Onesimus had done and was covering the possibility of theft. Others think he knew full well and was saying, 'If you insist on having the money back, let me pay it for him.' Did Paul have enough money to meet the cost? He obviously did not expect to have to pay. Philemon would have taken the teasing point in verse 19: 'You owe everything to me. I won't mention that.' (In so saying, of course, he does mention it.) 'So you won't really expect me to pay you back a few coins, will you?'

Onesimus might well have expected punishment. It would have been at the owner's discretion. In those relatively enlightened days the punishment would not be barbarous, especially as Philemon was obviously a warm-hearted man. Onesimus's life would not have been at risk. However, Paul is asking that Onesimus should be

▶ received back

▶ forgiven

▶ relieved of his debt

▶ accepted as a brother

What a remarkable parallel to the process of redemption proclaimed by the gospel! In fact, of course, this is one of the practical outworkings of that gospel. All this and more. Paul is confident that Philemon will do even more than he asks (verse 21). To continue the parallel, as Jesus said, 'Give, and it will be given to you. A good measure, pressed down, shaken together and running over, will be poured into your lap' (Luke 6:38).

Questions

1. What do you think Onesimus felt like as he delivered this letter to his master? Assuming that Philemon did as Paul requested, share your own experiences of being received by God, forgiven and adopted into his family. How far are they similar to those of Onesimus?
2. Should the local church receive all and sundry into its fellowship? What evidence of repentance should we expect, if any? Are references needed from reliable Christians?
3. Can those who have committed crimes or serious sins be received back as church members? Under what circumstances? Some churches do not operate on a membership basis. How do questions 2 and 3 apply to them?
4. What is wrong with slavery, if humanely practised?

Paul and slavery

In several of his letters Paul shows his concern that slaves should be well treated (see, for instance, Ephesians 6:5–9) and that Christian slaves should set a good example by serving their masters well. In this letter Paul comes near to suggesting that Onesimus should be set free; he should be treated as a brother by Philemon. Slaves could be freed at that time, and often were. But slavery as a system remained in place during the life of the Roman Empire, medieval and Renaissance Europe, and notoriously in the American colonies, fed by British traders, and in the USA until the nineteenth century. Slavery is by no means unknown in many parts of the world today, not least in the sexual exploitation of young women and children.

It was under the Christian influence of such men as Wilberforce, Shaftesbury and Fowell Buxton that first the slave trade and then slavery itself were officially abolished in the West, but it has often been asked why Paul did not take the logical step of denouncing slavery as contrary to God's will. It may be argued that the society of his time was not ready for emancipation on a total scale. But neither was it ready for the gospel, and that did not prevent Paul from preaching! Perhaps he saw it as a long-term outcome of the gospel, to be worked on by others while he concentrated on the core message from which all other good things would flow. At all events, this little letter makes Paul's point that slavery was no bar to equality in the sight of God. It is his broadest hint that therefore the whole system was flawed. It is ironical that it took another 1,800 years for the implications to be worked out, and that the world might so easily slip back into slavery again.

Philemon 22–25

Farewell

Hope for a personal visit, a warm farewell, love from the fellowship and a prayer for grace.

The final four verses look like a formal ending, but there are important matters here.

Philemon's hospitality (verse 22)

'Oh, by the way,' Paul seems to say, 'do have a room ready for me.' Philemon and the Colossian church had been praying for Paul's release. Did Paul know that, in answer to their prayers, he was about to be set free? Perhaps so. But how long would it take him to travel to Colosse? If he was writing from Ephesus, only a few days, but if he was in Rome, many weeks.

Paul could not be 'restored' to Philemon, as he had never been to Colosse. The word implies 'granted' or 'given as a gift'. His coming to them would not be a threat, like a spiritual inspection, but a delightful prospect. It would mean that Paul had been released from prison and would be able to enjoy fellowship with his Colossian brothers and sisters face to face.

Paul's greetings (verses 23–24)

'Everyone here sends their love,' Paul is saying. The five names that appear here are also mentioned along with others at the end of the letter to Colosse (see pages 99–101).

'*Epaphras*, my fellow-prisoner', appears to have been literally in prison with Paul, while the others mentioned were free. Of course, Paul may have meant 'fellow-prisoner in Christ' to mean 'co-prisoner-of-war in the Christian battle', but then why did he call the others by a different title, 'fellow-workers'? Epaphras was a native of Colosse and had brought the gospel to them in the first place.

Mark is probably John Mark, son of that Mary in whose house the fledgling church used to meet in Jerusalem (see Acts 12:12). He had been the companion of Paul and later of Barnabas on missionary journeys, and the cause of disagreement, even conflict, between them (see Acts 15:36–41). Mark seems to have come back into Paul's circle. He could well have been the writer of the second Gospel.

Aristarchus was a Macedonian from Thessalonica and was one of Paul's regular travelling companions (see Acts 19:29; 20:4; 27:2). In Colossians 4:10 he is described as Paul's 'fellow-prisoner', so perhaps he was behind bars too.

Demas is mentioned in Colossians 4:14 and also, some time later, more in sorrow than in anger, in 2 Timothy 4:10 as having forsaken Paul because 'he loved this world'. The

Bible does not gloss over the unpleasant facts that a triumphalist account might have omitted.

Luke is described in Colossians 4:14 as 'Our dear friend Luke, the doctor', and is well known to us as the author of the third Gospel and of the Acts of the Apostles.

God's grace (verse 25)

Paul has made a big demand on Philemon's resources of generosity, and he knows that his friend will need all the grace that God can provide to help him to respond. This is what N. T. Wright has called 'Christ-shaped grace' (*Colossians and Philemon*, Tyndale New Testament Commentary, p. 192). It is this grace that alone brings about reconciliation between master and slave and between God and his people. Thank you, Paul, for this delightful letter.

Questions

1. 'Philemon, elder of the church in Colosse, to my brother in Christ, Paul: greeting. Grace and peace be yours in Christ ...' Complete this imaginary reply to the letter we have just been reading.
2. How does your church fellowship keep in touch with members far away: those at college, mission partners, those working away from home? Plan a strategy of encouragement for them, including: who will write (and visit, if practicable), how often, who will pay the postage and other costs, how replies will be shared, how prayer for them can be encouraged, and so on.
3. What have you learned from your reading of this letter from Paul? Make a list. If anything on your list suggests possible action, how will you set about it?

From useless slave to bishop?

We have noticed Paul's liking for playing with words when he writes that Onesimus ('useful') had been useless but had now become useful again (verse 11). There is more to the wordplay than meets the English eye, however. In Greek, the language in which the letter was originally written, 'useless' is *achrēstos* (not useful) and 'useful' is *euchrēstos* (really useful). If this is not enough, it will be obvious that *chrēstos* and *Christos* are very similar words. Onesimus is now 'in Christ'.

There is an intriguing possibility that Onesimus later became a bishop! In his letter to the Ephesians, early in the second century AD, Ignatius mentions an Onesimus who was bishop of Ephesus. We have no way of knowing whether this was the redeemed slave, but he could have been.

The fact that the letter survived and was included in the New Testament suggests that it was received with due respect by Philemon. He didn't tear it up! We can assume that he agreed to Paul's request to have Onesimus back. Perhaps Onesimus was given the letter and kept it as a treasured possession. Then he offered it to the wider church as suitable for inclusion in the Scriptures then being collected. Who could refuse an offer like that?

For further reading

William Barclay, *Philippians, Colossians, Thessalonians*, Daily Study Bible (Saint Andrew Press)

Derek Tidball, *The Reality is Christ: The Message of Colossians for Today* (Christian Focus)

N. T. Wright, *Colossians and Philemon*, Tyndale New Testament Commentary (IVP)